1985

THE ACTOR'S EYE

THE ACTOR'S EYE

by

MORRIS CARNOVSKY

with
PETER SANDER

Foreword by John Houseman

PERFORMING ARTS JOURNAL PUBLICATIONS
NEW YORK

Morris Carnovsky, ca. 1929

for

PHOEBE

For information, write to Performing Arts Journal Publications, 325 Spring Street, Room 318, New York, N.Y. 10013.

Library of Congress Cataloging in Publication Data
The Actor's Eye
Library of Congress Catalog Card No.: 83-62614
ISBN: 0-933826-61-3 (cloth)
ISBN: 0-933826-62-1 (paper)

Graphic Design: Gautam Dasgupta

Printed in the United States of America

Publication of this book has been made possible in part by grants received from the National Endowment for the Arts, Washington, D.C., a federal agency, and the New York State Council on the Arts.

CONTENTS

ACKNOWLEDGEMENTS

A long time ago I shared a dressing-room with a peppery Scotsman with whom I had many energetic conversations, mainly about actors and acting. I once asked him tentatively about his own "approach" (that was the word I used) to a certain role. The word seemed to lash him into a small paroxysm of fury. This is the way the outbreak went:

He: (A very good actor, by the way.) Approach, approach! That's all you American actors think about, approach!! What about the page, the printed page? There it is in front of your eyes. Look at it—listen to the words, man, the words, then say them with all you've got, and that's all there is to it! Approach! (Murmur and gnashing of teeth.)

I: (Roused to curiosity, especially since he had placed his remarks on an international level.) You seem to suggest that you'd like us Americans to keep our dirty hands off of Shakespeare!

He: (Still puffing.) Yes, that's exactly what I do mean!

I was deeply committed to the study of Shakespeare at the time, so I couldn't oblige him. But I was touched by his protectiveness toward the Great Will, and recognized that fundamentally we shared the same passion, dirty hands or no.

I am grateful to that far-off Englishman for an illuminating experience that showed me there was more than my way of "approaching" Shakespeare. Nevertheless, there *is* my way, and that's what this book is all about—to remind myself of my own processes of digging and delving, to share whatever insights I may have gained with my fellow-diggers, and to remind them of their own voyages and discoveries. This is not a memoir or a how-to book, though sometimes it may seem to partake of the qualities of both. My hope for it is that it may touch off some of the excitement that it generated in us while it was being written, a sense of new discovery on fresh surmises, especially in the realm of Shakespeare.

Needless to add, I sense with gratitude the unseen presences of the many who hover about this work—teachers, fellow-actors, ever-abiding influences like Stanislavski and Michael Chekhov and Harold Clurman. Thanks to my Mother and Father who introduced me to the anguished culture of Yiddish Theatre. To my Wife who sees Eye-to-Eye with me in our common understanding of craft. To Gertrude, my sister, who transcribed the book. To my son Stephen who gave it its final shape. To the friendship of Matt Conley. To my former comrades of the Group Theatre. To John Houseman who summoned me to the world of Shakespeare. And—most especially—to Peter Sander, my interlocutor, who nudged, elbowed, and finally corralled me into the writing of our Book.

M. C.

Easton, Connecticut
September, 1983

Foreword

by

John Houseman

If any living American actor has a right—nay, almost the obligation—to give us his mature and deeply felt observations about the theatre from the contemporary actor's point of view, it is Morris Carnovsky. Very few Americans have had his wide range of professional experience: his career, in its fifty-year span, covers every major acting mode of our time.

Beginning in 1922 with his appearance in the Jewish theatre classic, *The God of Vengeance*, his record includes a seven-year spell with the Theatre Guild in its prime in a variety of plays whose authorship ranges from Lenormand, Shaw, Werfel, Sidney Howard, Pirandello, O'Neill, Chekhov, Philip Barry, and Maxwell Anderson. In 1931 he transferred his allegiance to the new-born Group Theatre and played leading parts in its productions of *The House of Connelly*, *Men in White*, *Awake and Sing*, *Paradise Lost*, *Golden Boy*, and *Rocket to the Moon*. With the dissolution of the Group he moved back for a time into the commercial theatre and appeared in such varied plays as *My Sister Eileen*, *Cafe Crown*, *The World of Sholem Aleichem*, and *Tiger at the Gates*.

In 1956, in his early sixties, he made yet another change. Joining the American Shakespeare Festival Theatre at Stratford, Connecticut, and beginning with modest roles (Salisbury in *King John*, the Provost in *Measure for Measure*, and Grumio in *The Taming of the Shrew*) he moved on, in his second season, to Quince and Shylock, in which he scored a resounding national success. In succeeding years he appeared as Claudius, Prospero, Malvolio, and his crowning triumph—*King Lear* in Connecticut in 1963 and, the following year, in California.

This impressive roster does not cover his long and honorable career as a director and teacher, nor does it include his work in the mass media where his film roles range from Anatole France in *Zola* in 1938 to Judge Julius Hoffman in B.B.C.'s famous documentary of the conspiracy trial of the Chicago Eight in 1970.

Few American actors can look back on such a range of achievement. But what is special and unique about Carnovsky is the intensity and depth of his personal commitment to each of these multiple incarnations. The fifty roles he played for the Theatre Guild, the Group Theatre, and A.S.F.T.A. were not casual engagements or temporary jobs. With each role, whether it was large or small, modest or flashy, he became an organic and passionate part of the production in which he was involved. Over the years he seems to have embodied the virtues (and sometimes the limitations) of most of the significant theatrical movements of our time; he absorbed and digested the techniques, theories and philosophies of each one in turn without ever losing his own dedicated passion for the profession of acting.

It is in the depth and wealth of these acting experiences that this work has its roots. As edited from the tapes of master-classes and interviews with Peter Sander of the Theatre Department of Brandeis, these are the opinions and convictions of a thoughtful and dedicated actor; always, for all their erudition, these are theatrical perceptions and reactions formed and viewed through *The Actor's Eye* which, quite appropriately, is the title of this very personal and fascinating book.

It is divided into two sections: the first—"Overview"—is an edited version of three master-classes conducted by Carnovsky for Brandeis theatre majors. The second half of the book, in which Carnovsky answers leading questions posed by Sander, is different in tone. In "Overview" Carnovsky, the teacher, is trying to clarify and stimulate among members of his class the actor's awareness of "self" which each one of them must develop and use in their physical and emotional contacts with "objects" that include their fellow students and the characters and situations of the play in which they are to perform. His exhortations are addressed to a vaguely aspiring audience of untrained and immature theatre students.

The "interviews" contain a more leisurely and subjective summary of Carnovsky's feelings about the theatre. He communicates them through the examination of a number of great roles, mostly Shakespeare's—those he has played and not played. Among the former are Prospero, Claudius, Malvolio, Shylock, Lear, and Falstaff. The latter include Juliet, Hamlet, Edmund, and Macbeth.

The Actor's Eye contains much implicit, autobiographical material: there are vivid glimpses of life within the Group during the Great Depression of the thirties and of the trauma of the Hollywood Witchhunts in the forties and fifties, of which Carnovsky was a victim. For my part, I found it interesting to read of his reaction to the offer I made him in the summer of 1956 of his first Shakespearean role:

> It was like plunging a magnet into a bunch of filings; the ideas surrounding the impulse to do Shakespeare began to coagulate and I immediately began to think in the terms to which I was accustomed—namely action, atmosphere, all the technical elements I had inherited from the Group experience.

This same process leads him, in the course of his "interviews," to some fascinating and original theatrical opinions. Of the Elizabethan soliloquy, for instance, he tells us that "in acting terms, it is the point at which the given circumstances collide with the actor's will and the character's 'spine.' The soliloquy comes as an attempt to sort it out."

Not all his observations are so technical. In his subjective summation of "the actor's function—his fundamental response to life," Carnovsky writes simply and with fervor of his life's work:

> Everything coming out of life to us is transfigured or transformed in the melting pot of our individual imagination, then goes forth in another form—an arranged and significant form. We're given the material to work with; we don't create it out of whole cloth. The material itself excites us. To the degree and in what form it excites you lies either success or failure. . . . You face a play by Shakespeare and it faces you as if to say, "Here I am. Put me on the stage. Make me come to life." It is a tremendous challenge! And you don't rise to it merely by studying the lines and putting the emphasis in the right places, but by mingling imaginatively with the whole life of the play.

In *The Actor's Eye* Morris Carnovsky speaks with the voice of an actor who has been doing just that throughout his professional life.

Preface

When I was a student, Morris Carnovsky came to speak at our college as he did at many campuses during his long career in the theatre. At that time I remember his saying, "There are many ways to act, but only one way to teach acting." He was referring to the Stanislavsky system. Subsequently I learned that there were also many ways to teach the Stanislavsky system. What Morris Carnovsky has succeeded in doing, however, is to distill the many elements of that system into three simple components: Self, Action, and Object, which permit the actor, student, and professional to look at his work from a greater perspective. While some of Stanislavsky's disciples took one aspect of the system and exploded it into a method, Morris in the simplest terms embraces the whole thing. But this simplicity is deceptive, for it is the essential simplicity of master artists such as Ibsen, Picasso, and, of course, Shakespeare, who have, through their trials and experiences, found the most economical, basic means of realizing their profoundest observations of reality.

In our interviews Morris constantly insisted that one should not be too dogmatic in the teaching or the learning of the craft of acting; that this "trinity" of Self, Action, and Object is not a mystical key to the actor's salvation. It is merely a way of looking at Stanislavsky's discoveries and of examining one's work in relationship to the play or the role at hand.

This book emerged from our working together on the faculty at Brandeis University where we both taught acting. I was excited by the inspiration that Morris generated among the students, and the clarity and articulateness of his approach to acting, Shakespeare, and the theatre in general. These are rare attributes in an actor, and there are very few books on acting that deal with techniques from an accomplished participant's point of view.

It was not until Morris returned to Brandeis in 1970 to appear as Falstaff in my production of *Henry IV, Part One* that the lectures were taped. We conceived of supplementing these lectures with a series of interviews which would go into further detail, drawing extensively from Morris's wealth of experience in the professional theatre.

What these lectures and interviews can only remotely suggest, however— what they can only hint at—is the sheer gusto and love of life that this man possesses. After our intense recording sessions, we would often walk, sticks in hand (sticks which more often than not were mementoes of one show or another) over the fields adjacent to his home in Easton, Connecticut. On the way Morris would pause to admire the color in a blade of grass, the moss on some rocks, the peculiar arrangement of some fallen branches, deer tracks, or simply the panorama from "the hill." And this attention to Objects is reflected in the classroom. The students may even have learned more from Morris's own devotion and respect for his craft—the love for the work and the students' gradual self-realization in it, and his enthusiasm for the material from Shakespeare they were exploring—than from the vital lessons in technique that he was imparting to them from his own experience. In this he was perpetuating what he himself had discovered, "The very examination of our capabilities as actors in the Group Theatre was an act of love. And fundamentally, that's how I still think about everything that an actor does with all his truth and depth. An act of love."

Peter Sander
Athens, Ohio

for Mary Jane

Lectures on Acting

As Aaron Katz in *The World of Sholom Aleichem*, 1953.

The following lectures were presented at Brandeis University between March 18th and March 28th, 1970, as an introduction to an intensive two-week course in acting for graduate students. The occasion for the course was Mr. Carnovsky's appearance on campus to play the role of Falstaff in my production of Shakespeare's Henry IV, Part One. *Soliloquies by Shakespeare were assigned to each of the class members, many of whom also had roles in the production, and these assignments formed the basis for work on and the discussion of the technique of acting. The lectures have been edited for clarity in reading. Comments and questions are italicized throughout.*—PMS

I

Now about this course: a two week condensed collision—in which I hope to transmit to you some of the principles that have guided me and still do in the preparation of any part. Obviously it is impossible; you can't make over people in two weeks, but we may receive a certain amount of stimulus if we remember, to begin with, that this is intended to be a practical approach. I will talk probably more today as a prelude than in the ensuing days; and if you take wise notes from time to time, I think you may be left with a little nugget of something that you can hang on to and perhaps use in your future work.

The first vital element in the makeup of the actor is the *Will*. Actors have to have strong Wills, and sometimes I get furious with myself for losing control of that same Will. It's terribly difficult and takes a lifelong practice to learn how to really concentrate on the matter at hand. Normally, I have a pretty good Will on stage. Off-stage, you can do anything you want with me—but on stage I do have a determination which comes from the understanding of what I want to do and the drive to achieve it.

When I'm disturbed in that first scene of *Henry IV* by the business of dressing which doesn't consummate itself properly, Will goes out of the window and I become a victim, not a dominator. This happens to all actors; but at such times one of the most important buttons that you must learn to push is the ability to summon up what power you have, to control your Will, to be able to say "this shall be" and lo, it is.

I always think of the actor as not only doing, but standing aside and watching what he is doing, so as to be able to propel himself to the next thing and the next thing and the next. And that again comes from a coolness, a kind of calm, in the heat of battle so that the actor may be able to command all of his resources.

You must be able to concentrate on the matter at hand in order to free yourself from the influence of the audience. The audience, of course, comes voluntarily; wanting to have a good time, wanting to understand what you have to give and tell them, but at the same time, their scrutiny of you can be destructive if you the actor allow it to be. I remember when I was playing at the Theatre Guild, in order to overcome this, I didn't know then what drove me to it, but I would go down on the stage before the rise of the curtain where I could hear the sound of the audience out there and I'd call them all kinds of dirty names. The whole idea was, "You're *not* going to have the power over me so as to destroy my Will to concentrate on what I have to do." Of course there are better ways of summoning the Will than that.

It is good to remember that nobody asked us to go on the stage. For my own part I elected to do so. And once having done that, it is for me to command all my resources by my Will, in order to prove my right to stand there and play.

I assume, since you are all graduate students, that you are well acquainted with the work of Stanislavsky: that you have read at least two of his books and that you know the story of his life, how he got together with Nemirovitch-Danchenko to form the Moscow Art Theatre. We don't talk very much about Stanislavsky anymore. He has often been dismissed as the arch-exponent of Realism in the theare, which has come to mean the photographic imitation of life: Naturalism. But in fact Stanislavsky was a poet with great imagination and insight, a commanding personality who aimed at more than mere Realism, who aimed at freeing the actor *completely*: his body, his mind, his imagination, his individuality, his morale, everything. There was nothing in the life and makeup of the working actor that Stanislavsky didn't take into account in his examination of how to make this machine function properly and creatively in the theatre. He strove for *Reality*, not Realism on the stage. There is a distinction. Reality applies to every period of theatre: to Shakespeare as well as Chekhov. The craft of the actor lies in how to be Real in the midst of given circumstances; and period and style are only two of the circumstances visited upon us as actors and which we must learn to control. The plays of Congreve, Shakespeare, Shaw, Odets are so different each from the other, yet each is filled with its own Reality.

Shakespeare, above all others, added another ingredient in the makeup and the necessity of the actor: Poetry, and by poetry I mean "flight." Shakespeare, I think, induces flight in the actor by means of his poetry. Without that flight, a Shakespearean play can fall dully about our ears.

How does a poet-dramatist convey the inspiration that seems to dominate a character like Hotspur, for example, a man whom we recognize as a hothead, a man who brings about his own downfall by his upsweep, so to speak? Well, I think in the same way that he conveys the character of Glendower, or Falstaff, and sometimes Henry. The language suddenly becomes thrilling. It is no longer prosaic. It has a physical character. It forces the body to be upright. It forces invisible wings to grow on the shoulders of the actor; and it's this that actually brings to life the style behind the playing of Shakespeare. I've had this experience for myself a number of times and what I discovered, very much so in the case of Shylock, Prospero, or Lear, is that the language almost urges me to rise up off the floor. As if it becomes impossible to hold myself down. For myself I'm particularly responsive to the sound of words but it is a quality which can be found, induced, studied, and finally inculcated in the work of all of you. There is something about the rhythm of Shakespeare's lines that makes an actor stand six feet tall. I've always held that Shakespeare is for demigods, at any rate, super-humans, not ordinary people. So these three characters in our play—Hotspur, Glendower, Falstaff, and I will include Henry in a way—have this peculiarity of darting off into the world of imagination. They become possessed; they become madmen, if you like. They are "essentially mad, without seeming so," and I think that is the center of what Falstaff means. Falstaff himself being "essentially mad, without seeming so," appreciates it when another person joins his company, in his "essential" madhouse.

Let me give you a more specific example from one of the soliloquies you will be working on during the course of our class. In that speech of Juliet's that you are preparing, you must think about caressing and chewing and digesting each word before you are satisfied with dismissing it. "Gallop. Apace. You. Fiery-footed. Steeds." What do you see? The animal's legs curving forward like waterfalls. "Fiery"—emitting sparks—images like that. You must not be in a hurry to say words like these. Speed works against you in the speech. Let it be speedy in intention, but not in performance. The excitement lies in those words, and words are particularly important to Juliet. Juliet is a person who suddenly pulsates with images—extraordinary images. She has an image-making facility. Juliet is a genius, a poet, as so many of Shakespeare's great characters are. She's passionate and that passion creates fountains of meaning, such as that sudden startling image: "When he shall die, cut him out in little stars, because even heaven will be jealous of the brightness and the luminosity of my love, my Romeo!" Juliet experiences a sudden dizzy vertigo that results in an image; to the degree that when Juliet in her potion speech sees such an image, she actually creates it bodily before her. "Stay, Tybalt, stay!" That's the poet's work, the poet's hand. So here's a girl who is on fire with the expression of love, namely through words and that's why "words, words, words" have to be loved and studied. One of the basic rhythms in *Romeo and Juliet* is the progress of Juliet toward womanhood—great, fulfilled womanhood. Her fulfillment comes not only by the act of love, but by all love, and the potential for her becoming a woman has to be noted in her earliest moments. When we first see her, she is an impatient, playful—almost childgirl, who has a will of her own, her own independence. Even though she says to her mother, "Whoever you choose for me will be all right, I'll bend to your wishes," that's not what she intends.

The theatre should be an *exciting* place. I feel impelled to say this to all of you so that our classwork will transcend mere pedagogy. It's not just a thing you work at, as you work at a sewing machine. You will get involved with *lives*, and here the most thrilling lives are provided for you by Shakespeare. I exhort you to bring your dreams to this little space here. It's not reasonable; I don't like reasonable acting. There is a place for reason in the theatre, of course, but that's largely the director's business. What we want in our actors is a kind of inner fire stirring, some kind of flame, as if, "I don't know what the hell I'm in this for, but it's great!"

Even by illustrating it, I am filled, as I talk to you, with this energy of flight and that's the kind of energy which should propel any play of Shakespeare, energy propelled in its turn by passion and imagination: passion that comes from wanting something to the exclusion of everything else. Imagination, well, that's God given, although to some extent it can be developed, secured, and nailed down by human sympathy.

But you can't just be crazy, "essentially mad," in the void. Paradoxically you have to have your feet on the ground in spite of the fact that I say you "fly." Your head, your imagination can fly, but your feet are rooted. When you come to a man like Shylock, he may want, in the last analysis, to be friends with the human race, to be friends with the Antonios of this world. He may want this, but he knows damn well that his feet are leaden as he traverses the streets of the ghetto; and he knows that the necessities of life in medieval Venice hang on him like a dead weight. And nevertheless, the collision of that fact with the equal fact of his desire to escape from that kind of life is what gives him passion, what animates the man.

What happens when the eye of our minds first encounters these extraordinary images that Shakespeare has created? If I were to say the names of these characters, one by one, to you, I have no doubt that you would immediately *recognize* them. I have only to say "Juliet" to you, and even if you hadn't read the play, nobody has to tell you what Juliet is about. I can see the recognition in your eyes. You *know* Juliet. Or I say "Richard the Third," again you need not have read the play, but you know that man; you'd recognize him in the haunts and alleys of England. I have mentioned the name of Shylock several times and though each one of you may have a different version of the image, nevertheless you know that man. Something in you responds. It's almost as if certain molecules in you were aroused and began vibrating in the direction of that image. And to that extent, you have an equal right with anyone to attempt the playing of those parts. But your apprehensions must stay alive and warm in order to continue to be in touch with the image which your own imaginations have aroused.

This whole matter of what we call identification with the image is the business of the actor's working to incorporate what he has *seen* in the eye of his imagination with what he can *do* in his own body, mind, and spirit. It's a kind of double activity. In first attempting Falstaff, for example, and certainly Lear, I would *look* at him: there he is out there, and sooner or later I know I am going to have to incorporate him into this body of mine. To be sure, with the help of the padding which I get from the costume department, but it's more than that. It's a spirit, something which I see out there and which I desire to merge with, and eventually hope will become one with me—a double activity: back and forth, back and forth. Even now I find myself pacing back and forth like, what?—a bear in a cage?, but that's the kind of energy and vivacity which is required of us when we face a character. Morris-Lear is different from Morris-Shylock or Morris-Falstaff. But they all come from the same shop. The creation of the role is not only induced by the quality of the image that we see, but we also impose our own qualities on the character itself as it emerges. Take the part of Blunt, for example; a very interesting quality in that man. His very name, Blunt, and the things which he stands for. Shakespeare did that on purpose and the kind of qualities which are drawn out of you in order to support your own image of Sir Walter Blunt is what's going to make the whole act of rehearsal interesting for you and assure and insure your place as a color in the whole composition.

If I am impatient with myself as Falstaff, it is because now, even in performance, he is not enough Morris. I know what there is in me which refuses as yet to come out into the character. But sufficient unto the day is the evil thereof. Nevertheless, I feel that there's not one of us (and since I don't exempt myself from this, why should I exempt anybody else?) there's not one of us who brings enough of *himself* to bear upon the character that he plays. That's no criticism, it's just something that I expect at the beginning. Incidentally, parenthetically, you know very well that we don't have enough time in the American theatre. There's where Stanislavsky had a great advantage. He realized that the act of creating for the stage took time and he was willing to give that time to the building of a character. We can't. We try to create under pressure. And that isn't really good for work.

You speak about an image you have in your mind of the character you want to play. Is acting a kind of imitation of the character or a creation of the character? Do you create an image in your head and then imitate it?

Coquelin, the great French actor, said, "When I study a part I learn the lines, I let them sink in. When I know the lines, I begin to create the character. I project him in front of my eyes. He's out there somewhere. I tell him, 'Here, you say these lines for me,' I listen to him and then all I have to do is imitate what he does. . . ." Now that's one way of thinking about it, but it really comes to the same thing. Because after all, the image that Coquelin projects out there and strives for comes out of Coquelin and nobody else. It's his own image after all, and whether he imitates it or not really doesn't matter; eventually it becomes his own flesh. Does the word imitation worry or bother you? Actually I don't think that we simply imitate anybody. For example, I see somebody in the street, a cripple perhaps, and I want to play Richard the Third—I have done this, I have followed people for blocks imitating their mannerisms—but on the stage it has to become my own. It has to emanate from my own legs, my own arms, my shoulders, and so on. We will talk more about this as we go along.

So, summarizing: Will; a conscious sense of reality or truth; and poetry; flight or energy that comes from passion and imagination, are pretexts that you as actors must bring to your work on the stage and even before that to your work on the whole technique of acting.

Now we come to the nub of the matter. I once made a kind of analytical map of the actor's work, allowing my mind to fly over all the important suggestions by Stanislavsky that I remembered: relaxation of muscles, concentration, communion, adjustments, line of action, through-line of action, Spine, all those things. I made an effort to simplify the whole task and I ultimately found, for me, that everything Stanislavsky was talking about in his monumental, lifetime work could be divided into three parts. I must confess that it does seem arrogant to try to huddle everything that a great man did and wrote in his lifetime into a simple formula, but this is the way I clarified it for myself. *I will say again and again that this doesn't exempt any of us from studying everything that Stanislavsky observed, wrote, or talked about.*

For myself, I came to this conclusion—that the unit of everything that happens on the stage is the Moment: the moment which is preceded and exceeded by another moment—one, two, three, four, five. Every moment can be examined differently from another moment. And the elements of each moment can be anatomized for the basis of this approach to Stanislavsky.

But first, in order to sort of wash our brains clear of dry talk, I want you to *do* something for me. I want you to relax. Deliberately relax. Everyone may take part in this. Continue what you're doing while I comment. This kind of relaxation could eventually, I suppose, lead to the happiness of sleep, but remember that we can't go to sleep on the stage. Nevertheless, we must still be relaxed. While you are practicing this moment of relaxation, keep it going by Will. Examine those portions of your body which seem not to be relaxed. If it's your shoulders, send them a message to let go. If it's the back of your neck, induce it to be relaxed. If it's the muscles of your face, very important, tell whatever tension is there to disappear. Don't lie back but pull yourself up and be attentive; maintain the *ease* that you are demanding of yourself. And again, say to the muscles on your face, give them the order, (not sharply, they will do it) "Relax." Now ask your eyes to let go. No, not to close. And again, ask them to be easy, easy. And perhaps by this time, certain little elements of tension would be intruding in your face muscles. Be aware of this and tell them to disappear, just to dissolve. This doesn't mean that you fall apart. Not at all. It simply means that you are getting into a condition where you can be most aware of your full readiness to perform tasks. But *recognize* the condition that you are in and encourage that condition constantly by relaxing your face muscles and your eyes. If any tension intrudes, throw it away. Command it to disappear. You don't need it. Keep it going while I tell you the following: that what you are now doing is a very creative thing. You are preparing your whole psyche, your whole mind and soul, to participate in a task, in something to take place on the stage. By your attention to me, at this moment, per- haps, you have incurred a certain tension of the eye. Tell it to go away. Easy. Easy. Everything very, very easy. And now will the members of the class, *maintaining this ease*, one by one, or two by two, go up on the stage, allowing this relaxation to permeate your bodies with the same particular kind of ease as you move. Go fluidly up on the stage. I will ask you to start simply to walk; to walk about the stage, maintaining ease. You're not zombies, you're not moving as if under hypnosis, you're moving pleasantly because it's good to move. Don't commit yourselves to moving single file. You can move anywhere. And when I say "stop," allow the impulse of movement to carry on even though your body has stopped . . . Stop! . . . Now, without movement, check your eyes . . . check your faces . . . check your bodies. If there are focuses or places of tension, dismiss them deliberately. This is where the Will can be employed. Command your bodies for the sake of the mind and the imagination, to leave yourselves free. And now move again. Just keep moving. You look very interesting to me now, very interesting. Keep moving, relax your necks. Be sure that you are very fluid. Relax your shoulders and again when I say stop, stop. Let the impulse to move continue in your mind, and . . . stop! And . . . continue. Place your feet on the floor significantly. Place them one after another, not merely shambling along, but because this floor is an important platform that your feet love to tread. At the same time inducing as much ease and relaxation as you can. That's right. Bumping into each other, simply adjust. Place your feet carefully on the ground, this wonderful space which can be inhabited by tragedy, com- edy, fairy tales, anything. This is a marvelous space. Be aware of it. Without being religious about it at all. This is your life, this is it. And . . . stop! Perhaps something more of an awareness of where you are will now seem apparent to you in the fact that you are placing your feet *significantly* on the floor. Now move forward again a little more quickly, and with more purpose, although the purpose doesn't have to be defined. Place your feet carefully. Don't shamble. Don't rush. Be aware that you are significant human beings. You are moving with some kind of purpose, even though it is not related to anything as yet. And . . . relax in the midst of it. Keep it up again when I say go. Go. And now with our faces easy and relaxed let us choose a circumstance. Let us simply move as if we were in some kind of joyous May Day parade. That's it. Let your eyes be relaxed. You don't all have to go in the same direction even though this is a parade. A little slower . . . and . . . stop. Keeping the impulse streaming from you, radiating *from* you. This is an act of concentration every bit as important and obvious, as evident as anything that you do on the stage. You are people who are *thinking* now, who are up there with a purpose even though it is the purpose which is given you by an author. It is rather general and vague but that doesn't matter. You are alive within it, and if you are not alive then you can invite more life by simply allowing your eyes to see more. Allowing your eyes to be free so that you will see other possibilities . . . and move forward . . . go. And now find each *other*; and when you find each other do so with all of the unself-consciousness that you have earned by this exercise. Just look at each other. Be with each other. Recognize each other's qualities. Without embarrassment, you are you, I am I, we are human beings in this together. Relax the eyes, —even now that technical thing can be done, and move slowly toward other partners, toward other objects. Recognizing each one as a human counterpart. Relax. The eyes. Even more and more. There is no limit to the amount of relaxation which you can induce in your eyes and in your thinking. And let me point out that as you are, what you have worked for, is *you* and nobody else. It's *you*. I repeat—you are *you*. Be aware of this sensation—check that sense of "I"-ness. Check it with your eyes and faces. Relish it. See whether your face does not carry out the simplicity of what you yourself are at this moment. Find other partners. It's too good to waste on just one or two. When we change there is apt to be that moment of slight tension which you will learn, must learn, you already have learned, to dismiss. You don't need it. Ease. Ease in relationships. Recognize this feeling in your bodies. Recognize that it is there. Ask yourself even, "how am I?" And recognize that feeling of readiness for anything, for action, for emotion, for anything. You have no idea how interesting you are at this moment. But that needn't tense you. Accept it as the necessary consequence of what you have worked for. Oh, yes, there are things which I am seeing which I have never seen in your faces before. And now, connect with each other in that same May Day parade. Greet each other. Be with each other. Go. Don't abandon what you've found. Be with each other. Command the relaxation in your eyes. We dare not be embarrassed on the stage. We dare only to take the life of the stage as our lives. Place your feet significantly, whether you dance or jump or hop or whatever it is. This is your space. Yes,—Yes! All right. And now maintaining what you have in your faces, in your bodies, go, each person to your seat down here.

****

I will ask you, were you acting?

I think acting is something that is more planned.

This *was* planned. I planned it for you. Well, I think you were acting. This is acting. This is what I think acting should be. At any rate, what the atmosphere of the feeling of acting should be. And in this way you will experience no distinction between behaving and acting.

So where is that image that you say was in front . . .

No, I didn't have any image. I wasn't working for that. Actually, if you like, I was working for the image of each person for himself.

But what I want to point out is that by my insistence on the "I," the personal feeling in the very midst of all the activity, insistence upon relaxing the muscles of the face, the muscles of the eyes, what I was inducing and suc eeded in achieving to a great extent, because of what you yourselves did, was to get down to the *"creative nub,"* if we may bring together a couple of odd words, of every person as an actor. That's why I asked you to be conscious of the fact that you were really relaxed, that you were really in a sense happy in your relaxation, that it became easy for you to *sense the possession of your unique selves.* And what I want to point out is that that sense, which I invited in you by exercise of your will, can be remembered and self-induced. Not by a species of hypnosis, I don't mean that at all. By conscious practice we learn to recognize that is the most *operative element in our equipment—ourSelves, which hereafter I spell with a capital "S." We shall call it the sense of Self, and it can be induced on the stage in the midst of action.*

To take a violent extreme of action, Othello strangles Desdemon? Never does an actor need more a sense of his own Self than at a moment like this because the very act is one of violence, of tension, but nevertheless, in the midst of that tension, as Hamlet puts it, "You must beget a temperance that will give it smoothness," and it's right there that the actor needs to use his own Self. Why? Because he deals in truth and no truth can be expressed except your own truth. That's where truth lies, in *your* truth. The way *you* do Othello will be different from the way anybody else does Othello. It will be *your* Othello, and it will be yours by the use of this sense of Self, simply by means of relaxation. And relaxation is something that you have just experienced up there on the stage. That's the thing in itself. People call it by different names. Michael Chekhov used to call it simply "feeling of ease," Stanislavsky, "relaxation of muscles." Stanislavsky once remarked that all his life he strove for true relaxation on the stage; and he said that only when he was about sixty years old did he find it. While I can't prove it because he didn't write further on that subject, I feel certain that what he found was himself within the character. Not the character within the Self, but himself within the character. As Richard the Third you can practice those very important and necessary contortions in order to get the feeling of a crippled man, but eventually it's going to be you within the cripple. And you will find also that when you do it, the sense of Self in you will be adjusted to the body which you have worked for. But you must be able to command your own "you-ness," if I may put it that way.

There are moments in Lear for example when, facing Goneril, I had to reach for, had to be in command of, an enormous rage; and the only thing that would give it to me would be relaxation—the sense of Self that we've been working for, plus the use of the Object.

II

Even with the exercise you've done, you have, perhaps you don't know it, a great key to Self-realization. I must tell you a story. Job hunting many years ago, I went to offices and saw these people sitting around, dressed to the eyes, you know—very stiff, very artificial, with their best foot forward—in their faces, so to speak; waiting for that electric moment, when the door would open, and out would come the director or his assistant who would say, "You, Mr. So-and-So will see you." The person summoned would get up and move with a kind of shellac all over him, trying to generate energy, coolness—all at one time. It used to sadden me very much when I saw this kind of nervous and tense behavior. It was awful, ghastly. And I said to myself at that time, "That, surely, is not what those people in casting are looking for. They don't want this, this galvanized corpse to walk through the door." Thinking it over much later, I daresay I myself suffered from this same kind of compulsion. I remember the feeling of immense relief when the stage manager or somebody came out and said, "That's all for today." Without even having seen "the great man" I was glad to have escaped down the stairs and into the open air. But I also found myself saying to myself: "Nobody has the right to make you put on a false exterior. No one has that right! No one in the world!" And therefore, I urge you to accept the only Self that you have.

When I was a kid, I made a damn nuisance of myself through an inordinate demand for sincerity. I used to accept or reject certain people because they either were or were not sincere. "I like her because she *is* sincere." You can carry that to an extreme, to a fault, too. But there is something to it. It isn't only the pursuit of sincerity. It's the pursuit of whatever you *are*. Accept it, strengthen it, have faith in it, and recognize its *signs*. Several of its physical signs you've already utilized in the exercise: the easy body, the easy face, the easy eyes. I would almost say that by doing the exterior bodily attributes first, you can induce the interior sense. But get the feeling—the feeling of being yourself. Know how to command it, that's the point. Know how, consciously, to say, I am all here. *I am I.* Know how to do that consciously. Even in the midst of Peto's activity, dashing about on that platform during the robbery scene, even in the midst of that, Harland can say, "I, Harland, am Peto." Or better: "I, Peto, am Harland." And thereby you may discover certain details, certain facets in the role that may never have occurred to you, that you didn't know existed because you hadn't found them in yourSelf.

No one can take away your Selfness. You don't have to be resentful of the other fellow because he may attempt to do so. Just say "I am I." That's all there is to it. "I am not going to jump over my own shadow; I am not going to be anybody other than myself." Not only is Self the final capstone on your feeling. It is your *power*. Your Self is your power. Which is a final reason for never allowing anybody to take it away from you—by insisting you behave otherwise than being true to yourself.

There is no one in the Universe exactly like you. No one. And therefore you have your own legitimacy. You are the king or queen of your own realm. You are it. *I am me*. The assertion of that fact in the midst of action, in the midst of anything that you as actors do on the stage is the secret of your power. I cannot emphasize that point too often. The use of the "I" is infinite; there is no extreme, no limit to its use and its power.

Let me touch on another inducement for developing a sense of Self: during that particular exercise I gave you, when people begin to be themselves and simply to relate to each other, a very touching thing happens. People become beautiful. It's the damnedest thing! The women become beautiful. And the men, drained of everything but their Selfhood, become extraordinarily handsome. So it's worth your while even on that level to achieve it.

At one point yesterday, I asked you, "were you acting?" and some people thought yes and others thought no. I could even say to you now, at this moment, "are you acting?" and I daresay the answer would be yes, and it would be the right answer. Even as you sit there in your very interesting and different ways, listening to me, each one of you backed up by your own peculiarities, your lifelong individuality, I want you to realize how completely unique you are. An extraordinary sight to me. I get very aroused and even touched by it. As you sit there, you are already realizing, and consciously, your own Selfhood, your Selfness, your own power. That's what you bring into this room. That's what you bring to the work on the stage.

The pleasure I personally get from looking at people who are listening and involved with me, as I am involved in this subject, comes from the fact that I see enormous potential for human good in a class like this. I don't want to go beyond the scope of what I'm here for, but that sense of Selfhood is not only the secret of power for the part or the play that we're doing, but, I feel, also for the good of the world.

I'll tell you something. At the last performance of *Lear* that we did in Stratford, we were all high, I tell you! Talk about a sense of Self, every person—we had played the play all through the summer; we were wound up in it, you know; and it was truly a thrilling performance, that last one. After it was over, I remember a young lady came back to see me and she said, "You must do this play all over the world because it will bring peace."

Now you laugh, but what she was feeling was a sense of harmony with us, a sense of fulfillment, a sense of "My God, the theatre is a great instrument. It's a great means of communication. The plays that Shakespeare wrote are profoundly humane, human. They go so deep you cannot resist them. They send you out thinking." This is what the woman meant, and I think she was celebrating in her being the arousal of her own sense of Self. I think this is what happens whenever we have any kind of great emotional experience. We become simplified. Into what? Ourselves. I am I. Why is it that when we go out after some great experience in the theatre or the concert hall or wherever, we don't chatter to each other. We don't want to say, "Gee, that was great," or anything of the sort. It's not necessary. It is because I think something has assisted us to reach a level of Self in our own experience which is unique. We're more than we were before. That is the purpose of art. To make the world of people more than it was before. That is the responsibility of the Self.

I had a letter from Ben Hecht, the playwright and journalist, who has since died. It was similar to this encounter with the young woman. He wrote saying, "I saw the play yesterday afternoon. I didn't applaud, but I went out afterwards into the grounds of Stratford. I walked down to the gate and suddenly I found myself turning around and going back; and I went into the theatre. There was no one in it, and I sat down in one of the seats and I said, 'My God, this is where it happened. This is where I saw it happen.'" He found it worth his while to communicate that to us. Again, you see, that was the kind of summons to Selfhood that Ben Hecht felt in himself.

I talk a lot about this because I want you to talk to yourselves about it. Sit alone, discover when you are most yourself. It is a very simple thing. It has nothing to do with the psychoanalyst's couch or with questions of mysticism. It has really to do with a state of being and the recognition of it.

I discovered and helped myself toward the Self in a very homely way—in the bathroom. I'd be shaving and since I've always either instinctively or by experience trained myself to be self-aware (I know, for example, at this moment that my hand is on my hip in a certain way, I sense that my body has shifted to this side, my toes supporting me on the other . . . I'm very much aware of my physical selfness, if you like), I suddenly said to myself, "Gee, I'm comfortable. I have no responsibility at the moment, just to shave." I realized: this is a good feeling. And I said "if now I can carry it from here out into the bedroom and then out into the kitchen, that same feeling, and then out into the street, no one can invade this sense of well-being. I could look into other people's eyes in just the same way as I look into my own in the mirror here, and it would feel good."

It's almost as if our bodies were peeled away and there, in the middle, is this thing which is absolutely unique. And we don't have to do anything about it. I don't have to say, "I am unique." Nonsense. I just am. It is amazing to be you at this moment and realize it, know it. And the thing for us to do as actors is to become *conscious* of it and exercise it year after year, moment after moment.

There are many things about myself that work against me when I am on the stage—some of the things I do in life out of habit. So doesn't some change have to take place when I'm on stage?

The change that has to take place is the matter of selectivity, as we call it, choice. There you are not altogether on your own, you are helped by your director, who points out the design of the part. Which doesn't imply that you sacrifice yourSelf for the sake of the design, you simply contribute those aspects of yourself which are good for the design of the part as the director and you agree to see it and understand it.

If you are in control.

Yes, artistic control means the intelligent management of what you're driving at—the imaginative perception, which will mostly be your own but will be approved by the director. And finally the assembly of all those qualities and many more within the actor who steps on stage and says, "Here I am." And that's the marvelous thing. I'm not obliterating the use of the intellect, the use of the mind. You need choice: *this* is good for the character; this is *not* good for the character. I choose to think about character as being the Self within the given circumstances. If Richard the Third, for example, is me, I then discover what his circumstances are. One of them is obviously that he is a cripple. He is tormented by his misshapen body. That I have to add to my circumstances; it becomes the circumstance under which I labor. But the person, the thing, that labors inside that circumstance is still *me*. Not you, not him, nobody else, just me. And one of the pleasures of being an actor is the discovery that your body is receptive and attentive to every demand of that kind that is placed on it, even in being crippled. There's a magic about the Self obeying the call of a character.

I think the question that they're asking is where does the Self stop and mannerism begin.

Mannerisms, I feel, can be very charming. I don't overlook them. Sometimes, in the theatre, people are cast for the sake of their mannerisms, as you very well know. They are often encouraged in the movies. When something like that is exaggerated out of all humanity, I think then it's bad. Just humanly bad. But I think about it this way: the sense of Self is a quiet thing. Quiet. It works while you sleep and it is proud. Stanislavsky talks about this when he describes something like the use of Action in *Building a Character*: "What we need are simple, expressive actions with an inner content. Where are we to find them? . . . If they (i.e. actors, dancers) would lend an attentive ear to their own mechanics, they would sense an energy rising from the deepest wells of their being, from their very hearts. This is not an empty energy, it is charged with emotions, desires, objectives, which send it pulsing along an inner course for the purpose of arousing this or that action. Energy, heated by emotion, charged with will, directed by the intellect, moves with confidence and pride, like an ambassador on an important mission. It manifests itself in conscious action, full of feeling, content, and purpose, which cannot be carried out in any slipshod, mechanical way, but must be fulfilled in accordance with its spiritual impulses."*

This Self is, as I say, proud, self-contained. Proud in no vain or egotistical way but simple. Objective. Receptive. I repeat, it is quiet. It is loving. It's ready. It has nothing to do with the jerks and distortions of the individuality. It *is* the individuality. Even in spite of mannerisms, if you can learn constantly to check how your Selfhood feels, if you can capture the sensation of what that is consciously, and learn to control it too, "turn it on" as it were, you will know the difference then between Selfhood and mannerisms.

And as a matter of fact with more use and realization of the Self, you become more original. You find out your way of doing things without ever destroying what the author meant or the director may intend—and it will be real. It's what Stanislavsky was talking about when he said "true actions in the midst of realized circumstances."

Recognize that this command can be technically controlled. This summoning of a fundamental quality in yourself can be done *on stage* in the midst of all of the interruptions and the tensions of performance, awareness of the audience, and so on.

And don't misunderstand me. This has always happened in the past; people have often said, "Yes, but I don't know my Self. I'd have to go to an analyst for ten years and spend the rest of my life on a couch." It has nothing to do with that. That's why I am careful to bracket the word "relaxation" with sense of Self. That's really all it is; it's full, vital, *interior* relaxation. You'll go home and practice it and make certain mistakes and begin to criticize yourselves—don't. Just keep on giving yourself the simple command to relax with special attention to your faces and your eyes, and your hands and your feet, the pleasure of placing your feet down on the floor and at the same time keeping the consciousness going in the head, knowing that you're doing this—consciously. If you simply practice it ten times a day, just by moments, you'll be doing what you are supposed to be doing as actors, because along with it will come moments of power—a sense of "Gee, I can do anything. I can build bridges. I can play Shakespeare. I can do anything." When you see a whole stage load of actors who are aware of their power without saying, "Look at me, how powerful I

---

*Stanislavsky, Constantin. *Building a Character*. New York: Theatre Arts Books, 1949, pp. 46-47.

am," who nevertheless relate to one another gently, simply, as you did in our first exercise, that is power. When you see a whole stage load of people like that, then you've got something. You've got relationship; you've got vital, significant *connection*.

III

The very next thing then to discuss, apropos this word "connection," is *the Object*. I have introduced this class to the word Self as I understand it, and we will probably talk a lot more about it, but Self cannot live by itself. "It is not good," says the Bible, "for a man to dwell alone." What it requires is an Object and we are surrounded by them: this unique Self in the midst of a world of Objects. The eyes that I spoke of before require something that they may encounter. I take pleasure, for example, in the simple tranquility of just looking, in encountering the obstacle which is *you*. And I hope it's pleasant for you to encounter this obstacle in the person of me. And that circle which is set up between us of looking, encountering, meeting, connecting, is of the very essence of acting on the stage. There's *pleasure* in that. There should be pleasure in all our technical means and devices. This is all technique, by the way. Why technique? Because it's conscious. Because it is something that we can learn to do. We don't *look* carelessly on the stage. That's not done except for a specific effect. We look. We perceive. We connect. Deliberately. That moment when Prince Hal says to me as Falstaff, "Do thou stand for my father." That moment . . . "Shall I?" You know that moment. What a radiating and expansive idea that is! Stand for his father? Shall I? In that moment the eyes of my mind encounter the *Object* of me putting on Henry the Fourth's crown, robes, everything. It isn't full. It doesn't need to be exact. We needn't torture ourselves with the exactitude of it, but in that moment I see Hal's father and I say, "Oh, yes! I'd like to be him," that's what gives me pleasure as Falstaff—the encounter with that Object. By the way, you may have noticed that I myself (it may be a fault) act a good deal out front; maybe it's because I'm nearsighted, I don't know. I may not always seem to connect with you as the Object; nevertheless, I have you in my mind's eye. Eventually I do come back to you, and you may be sure I'm always aware of you.

Well, Objects are of all kinds. You may think of our inner eye as being confronted by a series of images like those you have in film—one after another. Our eyes are always encountering something, whether a person, a thing or a thought or a memory of a vision or a fantasy or a suspicion or whatever it is. Everything that the eye of the mind encounters is an Object. And for the actor, the Objects that he chooses consciously are the ones that are going to stimulate him through the whole part. Take a moment I am particularly fond of referring to: Hamlet's moment when Horatio comes in to tell him that he has seen the ghost of his father and suddenly Hamlet says, "My father!—methinks I see my father." Horatio says, "Where? Where my Lord?" And he answers, "In my mind's eye." That is the act of seeing. That is an act of the Self encountering an Object—very, very frequent in Shakespeare and in life. Incidentally, making use of an old Hebrew saying, "Charity saveth from death," I substitute, "The Object saveth from death." Because as long as your eye, I mean it in both senses, e-y-e and "I," is encountering something, no matter whether it's a person or a thought or a memory or whatever, you are *alive* on stage. "The Object saveth from death." We actors say "we get something from" certain things on the stage; you receive what you can from the Object; and correctly considered, no man of sensitiveness, certainly with the sensitiveness of a Hamlet, would relate to the image of his beloved dead father with anything but the profoundest tenderness.

I'll tell you what; let's do another exercise, class; go on stage and look for Objects. Each one of you for yourself. Let us say, you are in an Indian temple. Now you have never been there, probably. Create it. Let me see it. Go into the temple and simply look at Objects, but be sure that you see them. Just walk about from one thing to another and look. You can even handle some of them if they are small enough or stroke them or whatever you like. Now each person, of course, is going to create a different kind of environment. And, in fact, it needn't be an East Indian temple, it can be a mosque or cathedral or whatever you like, but I want you to see the Objects. Also when you look at an Object, whatever it be, note that the eye itself becomes connected with it. Just let that little transaction between yourself and the Object be sufficient. If the Object is bigger, same thing. Deliberately, consciously utilize this connection, this principle which I told you about. Allow the Object to have potency for you. Don't adjust your faces; just allow what happens inside to happen. You know it's an act of love in a way, this falling in love with Objects, going from one Object to another. There is a reverence for what can happen between ourselves and the Objects we are surrounded by. Simply allow your eyes to find the Object and realize that because you have found that Object you are alive. You live. I'll say it again: "The Object saveth from death." So let your fancy roam. Walk around this place, this temple, mosque, synagogue, or whatever, find things and consciously, lovingly, connect with these Objects.

****

And so, by releasing oneSelf, as we have done, and relating to an Object—making the vital connection with an Object, we make conscious adjustments to every moment on the stage. This, briefly stated, is the second aspect of the whole Stanislavsky system that at least in my own experience, I have found, works. As I said before, I want this to be a practical course. So now we have the Self, represented by a capital "S," and the Object, represented by a capital "O."

Now there's no question but that two people encountering each other as Objects can spend hours without strain, except that with the passage of time it would become difficult just to keep looking with no purpose whatever other than memorizing each other's face. You can do that. But the actor requires an *Action*. What *happens between* the two Objects? What *happens* between me and you? What *happens* between me and a memory? What *happens* between Hamlet (me) and the image of the Ghost? What *happens* there is the important thing. And it is in the repercussion from Self to Object that the excitement of *the moment* is generated.

Here again Shakespeare makes that kind of greater demand on us. Shakespeare rarely requires the tranquil looking in the eye. Rarely. The moment is always *gorged* with activity, possibilities. Why? Because Shakespeare's actions are very strong, and they have to do with resolving conflicts. Imagine the encounter at the end of the play between Othello and Iago. There is not much to be said. Iago has just been unmasked and Othello realizes in that moment that Iago has brought about all the dreadful events of the play, that moment is every bit as important in its repercussion as the moment when he moves to kill Iago and is prevented. The *quality* of the "ocular" relationship between Othello and Iago at that moment is as tragic as anything in the whole play—that of realization. The Italians have a wonderful word, "rimbombare," which means "to rebound." It suggests molecules rebounding one from another. We actors have to agitate ourselves like those molecules in order to become exciting people on the stage, in order to come to Shakespeare's work with wings on and assume the responsibility of flying. Otherwise stay home. Shakespeare didn't ask you to be an actor. You wanted to. We must find ways of agitating ourselves, getting viscerally involved, of realizing that the world of Shakespeare is the most exciting world that has ever been put down on paper. *That's* what makes for excitement in doing these plays. There's no casual, tranquil air about Shakespeare. Only rarely. For the most part it has to do with strong wills, strong seeing, strong hearing, strong reacting.

I think all Action is violent in its basis. All Action. And in Shakespeare the Action is almost always fundamentally violent. And so between this same Self that we were talking about and this same Object, there pulses this back-and-forth Action, or, as you might prefer to call it, "trans-action." Because in my encounters with you, it's not only what I say that affects you, but what you say affects me, and what I expect you to say may be different from what you finally do say and that's what makes the scene too. It's a pulsing—a pulsing back and forth. Rimbombare. And that, as a matter of fact, is the whole thing in a nutshell: *Self*, *Object*, combined by given circumstances and propelled by *Action*.

And again, people, don't take this as a kind of quick dose of talent. Nobody can give you that, even by the application of the whole of Stanislavsky's method, as we know it. The three elements that I have talked about so far are based on my own experience of facing up to his design which I know is complex and complicated, but which is necessary to study part by part from beginning to end. That sounds like an involved task, never ending. But if one, for in-stance, has to spend weeks or months on the simple element of talking, then you do it. You must take time. An actor's time of study in fact should be coexis-tent with his life. While I'm on the subject, one of the things that I find very often is that actors indeed don't *talk*. They orate. They begin by putting the cart before the horse, to give results in terms of speech instead of simply trying to find out what it is they're talking about. It is necessary for you as actors to discover talking is simple communication—the desire for you to understand what I mean, and my desire also to get from you what you mean. This is no dif-ferent from ordinary simple verbal communication that we practice in our daily lives except that we must do it on stage. Once we step up here on this magic space we mustn't relinquish our humanity and proceed to be dummies or store mannequins. Learn to talk. It seems almost absurd to say anything about it because communicating with each other as I am doing now is accomplished very readily in life, but with much more difficulty on the stage. Therefore talk-ing is an essential result—a by-product, in a sense—of our fundamental pro-gram in this course. The connection between the Self and the Object by means of Action leads to the right kind of talking. When that connection is in any way deranged, then you have not been talking for the sake of conveying the purpose and the intention of the scene, but for the sake of making an effect, of hearing yourself speak. And this is a departure from the truth.

In these soliloquies and monologues you have been working on you're not absolved from talking. You're either talking to yourself, to the other person or persons in the scene, or in some cases (very strongly in the case of the Juliet po-tion speech, for example) the address is directly to the images that are created. Ease in talking comes to you gradually with experience, but it should be grasped now. Again from my own experience, if I ever feel, "Hold on there, man, you're not talking," the first thing I do is find an Object on the stage, whether it's a dagger that I'm using for a scepter, as in the case of Falstaff, or a table, or a person, or whatever. I find an Object and I make certain that I'm anchored to it mentally. Once more, "The Object saveth from death." Or to put it more positively, "The Object giveth life." And also it calls on the Self. *I* see you. I *see* you. I see *you*. I see you. And that in a way expresses the basic reality of our method. Eventually it all comes together, and this is the reason why I have analyzed our actor's work as a succession of moments. The Moment on the stage; one after another; which can be analyzed and realized in the light of these three fundamental elements—the Self, the Object, and what grows be-tween them, the Action.

When you are playing a part and you have a good strong consciousness of Self, how much of that is affirmed by the Object? What does the Object do for the Self?

It affirms it. You used the right word. At this moment, if I had a scene to play with any one of you, my realization of you and "your you-ness," so to speak, would at the same time affirm and confirm my own realization of myself so that that produces the richest kind of interactivity; when two people are connected by means of mutual realization leading to Action, or if you prefer, intention.

Let's put this whole thing to the test now by looking at some of the work that has been assigned. Very often in Shakespeare the whole of a character, its essence, can be perceived in his soliloquies, almost every one of them. Although they are not all alike, practically all of Hamlet's soliloquies indicate his character. There's not a soliloquy of Macbeth that doesn't reveal the fundamental essence of Macbeth. It's a very concentrated form. And so it allows the actor, since he is alone onstage, to grapple with his character's problem in himself, and this makes soliloquies very active, *packed* with action.

Edmund's first soliloquy from *Lear* is a perfect case in point apropos the matter of Objects.

> Thou, nature, art my goddess; to thy law
> My services are bound. Wherefore should I
> Stand in the plague of custom, and permit
> The curiosity of nations to deprive me,
> For that I am some twelve or fourteen moonshines
> Lag of a brother? Why bastard? Wherefore base?
> When my dimensions are as well compact,
> My mind as generous and my shape as true,
> As honest madam's issue? Why brand they us
> With base? With baseness? Bastardy? Base. Base?
> Who in the lusty stealth of nature, take
> More composition and fierce quality
> Than doth, within a dull, stale, tired bed,
> Go to the creating a whole tribe of fops,
> Got 'tween asleep and wake? Well then,
> Legitimate Edgar, I must have your land;
> Our father's love is to the bastard Edmund
> As to the legitimate; fine word,—'legitimate'!
> Well, my legitimate, if this letter speed
> And my invention thrive, Edmund the base
> Shall top the legitimate. I grow; I prosper;
> Now, gods, stand up for bastards!

(King Lear, I,ii)

I proceed by asking questions . . . How long have you, Edmund, been planning this step? How long have you suffered from this condition that you describe? The fact that you suffered from this all your life means that there is far more going on here than you say. In a way the character is similar to Shylock, because the indignities, the offenses that he has borne, the conclusions which he has drawn, and the determinations which he has made, have accumulated in him, in the back of his mind. Where, for example, did Edmund come to the conclusion that nature was his goddess? In a way that's the premise, you probably sensed it, of the whole speech. Yes, it has the quality of an invocation. What is nature? You say a goddess. What does she look like? Voluptuous, you say. What kind of eyes? *Where* is she? This dominating creature with the fiery eyes and the voluptuous bosom? Is she large? I only ask you these things in order to specify, to make you specify what you see. This is an example of the use of the Object. The first. Powerful. Now who are you going to relate this whole speech to? Who are you talking to? You say "*Thou*, nature, art my goddess." Is the whole speech to her? And by the way, before we leave the image of her, go as far as you like in your understanding of the essential nature of this woman: obviously a powerful woman, who dominates, infiltrates, and guides all of your actions. Now who do you talk to? You begin by invoking her. "To *thy* law my services are bound." Does she appeal to you? Does she encourage you? Are you her darling boy? Yes, I think so. There's a definite relationship between you and her. That's the kind of idea, by the way, in the area of the Object which can stimulate and agitate the actor. I know myself if I were playing Edmund, I would certainly use it, because it's organic to the speech. If I may make a general criticism I would have to say that what you did was casual and conversational, good enough, intelligent enough, but nowhere near the Edmund of the play. Why? Because it wasn't organically and agitatedly enough involved with the Objects. For example, you take a thing like "Base, base, base. Who said Base? Bastard!! Who invented such a word? Bastard!! A bastard??! Huh! What the hell's the difference—Bastard and legitimate? Why? Stupid mankind to invent . . ." I'm paraphrasing, of course. I'm going to greater lengths than are perhaps necessary but all of this is fermenting in Edmund's brain. He's an angry man. It started by his being angry way back when he was a kid, when Edgar got the best bicycle. It's the accumulation of fury in him that is controlled and mirrored in this particular speech. And so I ask you again. Where are your Objects? Nature is one. The letter in your hand is one, but it's a subsidiary one. Who else is he talking to? Is he talking to Nature throughout? What is it that would agitate you? To begin with, I think you would be agitated if suddenly a gorgeous, semi-nude figure of a female would arise and come to you and say, "Thou art my boy." And that's the kind of stimulation that we ourselves must bring to the work of acting! Imagination! And so it goes on. That's the first image. What I am trying to get out of you (it would take too long to pursue Socratically) is simply when you say, "Why should I stand in the plague of custom?," it's no longer Nature whom you are addressing, it's under her shadow that you speak, but now you turn your attention to the world. "All you decent, legitimate bastards out there, tell me, why should I stand in the plague of custom?" And so on. "All right, so I have a plan. And if it *kills* me,

I'm going to see it through." I want to point out, by the way, that all the characters in *Lear* are *doom-haunted*. They're all tragic. Lear's not the only one; Cordelia; Goneril's tragic; Regan's tragic; Edmund's tragic. The Fool. Why? Because each of them is the creature, the victim of his own fundamental necessity. The Fool cannot help but die for his master. It is the necessity of his being. Goneril cannot help being the sinister creature that she is. She desires power and love so much that her "fate cries out and makes each petty artery as hardy as the Nemean Lion's nerve," as Hamlet says. And it's the same with Edmund, now, in this speech: "I cannot help it. I must be all-powerful. I must top my legitimate brother."

And this induces, friends, maybe a different kind of look in the eye. I watch for those looks in the eye. That's why I say the Self, which I concentrate in the eye, e-y-e, of the actor, is an infinitely excitable and agitatable thing. And the eye shows it. Maybe I'm talking wildly here, but I conceive of Edmund as having red eyes. Of course, they're *not* red, but they're glowing with fever of the desire to dominate. It's a kind of sickness in Edmund. Just as the nature of Goneril is an infection. You recall Lear says to Goneril, "You are an infection in my corrupted blood." The whole play seems to smell of corruption. I'm not talking simply to show how I feel about the play, but in order to agitate your quality, your whole makeup onto the *level* of playing a supreme tragedy. No longer will it be possible for you to be casual about it and say, "Well, I'm kind of ambitious, you know, and I don't really see any difference between illegitimate and legitimate," instead of responding to the burning fire in him, this desire, this Action. And there we have it. Object, Action, You. Object, You, Action. "I will have it; I must have it. I'll die if I don't get it." That doesn't mean that you must produce this result immediately. I don't ask that. I only ask that when you study the speech at home tonight or whenever, don't speak it aloud, think of yourself as sitting in a corner dreaming up the possibility of the ultimate ambition that he "suffers" from. All of Shakespeare's villains have a kind of family resemblance. Richard the Third says in *Henry VI*, he is "like one caught in a thorny wood," you remember that? "And from that torment I will free myself, or hew my way out with a bloody axe." It's the same for Edmund. It's the fever of the ambition from which he desires to be free. The end of tragedy is freedom. After everybody has died, the world can breathe again. Sometimes this freedom is gained by suicide. The whole course of the trajectory of *Richard III* is one big act of suicide. He can't help himself. And with certain character differences it's the same for Edmund.

Now—the main Objects that you relate to are going to be Nature, the people that you talk to, even though they are not seen, and Edgar; and also, by the way, the *idea* of illegitimacy. That too is an Object. If you don't play it, you miss everything. Illegitimacy, that's an Object. And it depends how you, the actor, relate to these things that eventually makes Edmund fall within the circumstance of bitterly attacking the conventions of the world. You are not a man who retires from life. No, you are born to fight. What matters is your thinking about it, your ruminating about your dream, your desire to reach the level of a man who suffers and plans tragically for his own downfall, because he's bucking society, bucking everything. And he's bound to fall.

While we're on the subject of *King Lear*, let's see your Goneril speech. (Student does the scene.)

> Not only, sir, this your all-licensed fool,
> But other of your insolent retinue
> Do hourly carp and quarrel, breaking forth
> In rank and not to be endured riots. Sir,
> I had thought, by making this well known unto you,
> To have found a safe redress; but now grow fearful,
> By what yourself too late have spoke and done,
> That you protect this course and put it on
> By your allowance; which if you should, the fault
> Would 'scape censure, nor the redresses sleep,
> Which, in the tender of a wholesome weal,
> Might in their working do you that offense
> Which else were shame, that then necessity
> Will call discreet proceeding.
>
> This admiration, sir, is much o'the savour
> Of other your new pranks. I do beseech you
> To understand my purposes aright:
> As you are old and reverend, you should be wise,
> Here do you keep a hundred knights and squires;
> Men so disorder'd, so debosh'd and bold,
> That this our court, infected with their manners,
> Shows like a riotous inn: epicurism and lust
> Make it more like a tavern or a brothel
> Than a graced palace. The shame itself doth speak
> For instant remedy; be then desired
> By her that else will take the thing she begs
> A little to disquantity your train,
> And the remainder that shall still depend,
> To be such men as may besort your age,
> Which know themselves and you.
>
> (*King Lear*, I,iv)

Is this your heart's desire of Goneril? You yourself—what do you *want* of Goneril? What do you expect? If you were going to the theatre, and were told "I am going to see a Goneril! And *what* a Goneril I am going to see!," what would you expect? All right, a Fury; uh-huh, I see what you mean; how do you get that? How do you work for that? What are the qualities of a Fury? Whom are you hurting? Whom are you actually hurting by this outburst? Of course, you're hurting Lear, but who else? Yourself! Yes. Violence is something which is a double-edged sword. It may be pleasurable for a while, but it really hurts at its source. And yet you cannot stop yourself. I don't care to what extremes you carry it. You can shriek; you can yell; you can tear your hair. Eventually all that can be toned down. Again as I said before in the case of Edmund, it's a matter of achieving the level, in this case, the *level* of the Shakespeare tragedy. I think that unbridled fury or anger really hurts the person who practices it, and you know from your own experience when you yell at your own father or your mother or whomever, that something in your nature is going to make you say, "Jesus, why did I have to do it that way?" "And yet, goddammit, I'll do it again and again!" So the level that I'm talking about is the thing to be attained. And I don't want you to yell simply for the sake of yelling. Get it from a source. Get it, in other words, from yourSelf in connection with an Object.

Now I'm going to do something here. I'll simply from time to time remind you of Self, use the word "Self" to you. You do the speech again. "Not only, sir," and so on; and remember, think about the Fool and all that, and begin the speech at whatever energetic level you can. And I'm going to, from time to time, simply mutter or murmur the word "Self," and at that moment, remember when we were walking about and stopped, we kept the impulse going and then resumed the walk. Well, when I say "Self," stop, (this is an exercise, you know) stop, keep the impulse of the speech going, but say, "I am I. In the midst of this Goneril thing that I am doing, I am I." And then go on.

Do you want me to say it out loud that I am . . .?

No, say it to yourself and place it in your eye. I know this is a helluva lot to ask of you. If you can relax your eyes, let your whole impulse and action come through your eyes. When I say "go," continue; and I'll say "Self" from time to time. All right. I want you to be outgoing to the Objects. I want you to be aware that this outgoing is coming from a source and that is why I am softly urging you to remember Self, reminding you that not only is the Object bringing this out of you, but that you are also producing it. That moment then becomes a fulfilled thing when Self and Object meet.

****

I have been improvising around these soliloquies by paraphrasing the lines. Paraphrase enables us to cope with the naked meaning and action underlying all the words. Our own words need not and will not be as beautifully chosen as the original. But in their very coarseness, they may invite our intimate involvement in *what's* happening. For example, Hamlet's "Oh what a rogue and pea-sant slave am I!" He is saying, "I've got to think this over now in order to find out what to do! What to do! My God, it's a prodigious question! What the hell to do; it's shattering! But look at him—that actor. *He* knows what to do. He, 'this player here,' he has his craft. He knows what to choose so as to bring about the effects he wishes; 'yet I, a muddy mettled rascal,' what to do? I know! The play!" After the heat and fervor of the questioning is over, *that's* what to do!

This is a magnificent speech to work on again and again all through your life, because it will feed you. Actors find out ways of feeding themselves all through their careers. I recall in my own case, if I may, I was playing a fairly diminutive part in a play called *Men in White*. I was a doctor in rather sad circumstances. And for some reason before I'd go on, I chose to say the lines of Hamlet's solilo-quy, "To be or not to be." Now I was always intensely moved by it because there is inherent in it a choice—to live or not to live; and this had a bearing on the doctor that I was playing. Now the Hamlet speech had nothing to do with the play we were doing. And nevertheless, in a determining way, it did. I was able to arouse my own juices, so to speak, so that they were functioning on a higher level. And I was ready then to cope with the material of my scene, which was richer as a consequence. So as I say, this "Oh what a rogue" is one of the speeches that is so rich in the bodying forth of our fundamental "theorem": Self-Action-Object, that it needs to be studied again and again and again. In-cidentally, you don't always have to speak a speech like this aloud. You can think it through or say it through silently, examining the Objects in the speech. You might find that because you've absolved yourself of the need to speak, your reaction to the images is much more personal. And there is where you find emotions. We don't haul them up by violence. Very rarely. We woo emo-tions, lay traps for them, and our fundamental design here is intended to help you do just that. If emotion doesn't come, all right. Don't worry. It'll come some other day, but as Stanislavsky says, "It is not necessary to play greatly, it is necessary to play correctly," and correct playing is, if anything, related definitely to our basic "theorem." One can't be deeply moved all of the time, though there's a lot to cry about in this life of ours and now and then, blessed-ly, a lot to laugh about. One of the things which I'm almost afraid to mention, which is deeply moving to me, is the response of the audience, if they have been seized and are *with* you. That peculiar seal that takes place between audience and actor, when you create, is a shattering thing to me; it's also reassuring. It tells me that I'm not dead. Those intense and vibrant feelings which we are in-clined to be ashamed of exhibiting in daily life are the very things that warrant the fact that we can say we are alive, on stage or off. When I had you look at each other, connect with each other that first day, walking about, you recognized each other as people capable of this vibration, this constant living excitement.

Without audiences, nothing; we speak and act for them. But, if you allow them to come into the forefront of your mind as we actors are prone to do, it's apt to be an inimical factor in your work and your technique. On the other hand, if you learn how to assign audiences their proper place, they can be of inestimable help. Many of the things that have developed even in the course of this week of playing Falstaff have come from listening with that third ear to what the audience suggests. By the way, there lies danger too. Some of us, including myself, have fallen for it already, even in this week. We have become conscious that there are laughs imbedded in a scene and we court them, we woo them. We make that our Action instead of playing the Action of the scene. That's a sin. I don't know if it's a mortal or a venial sin. If it's a venial sin, I suppose God will forgive us; but at the moment it seems to me like a mortal sin, when it happens. When I catch myself saying, "Oh, look at me, ain't I cute," I hate myself. That's mortal. A little voice tells us very much about the wrong things we do, but the fact that we recognize them as wrong means that we know otherwise, that we know the true way. For instance, you may have a tendency to play for charm; and in a way the character you play, Prince Hal, lives for charm. Well, charm is a very necessary ingredient in the theatre. Stanislavsky said so, very definitely; so did Michael Chekhov. But if one plays for it, then it becomes a result that becomes detestable eventually. The Beau Brummels of the theatre are legion, they sell like hotcakes, but it's a question whether one wants to devote one's life to that. That is certainly not what I mean by Self. Charm is only an ingredient, and a very attractive one, of acting.

It's confusing, getting yourself going again when you know you're Prince Hal in relation to Falstaff but you're also yourself in relation to the audience.

More important is your relation to Falstaff. More important to me is Falstaff's relation to Hal. Much more important. The relaxation and joy of playing is what, you may be confident, produces the effect on the audience. The joy of this collision between Hal and Falstaff, between Poins and Falstaff. That peculiar "rimbombare" is what makes the audience enjoy it, and you must be confident that it does. We don't need to encourage them, to say, "Here you're supposed to laugh, to be delighted." No, no. We can be confident in the circumstances, in the game, because it *is* a game. This whole play is a game—sometimes a lethal one, it culminates in the piling up of bodies—a deadly game!—but along the way the game between you and me, between Poins and me, and so on, has an innate charm. You can feel Shakespeare's delight in discovering it. He needn't have included this "villainous, abominable misleader of youth," this Falstaff, as he chose to call him even though there was the accepted story about Prince Henry giving his youth to boisterous and riotous companions. But what a happy invention! And it works. It's bound to work. You're skinny and I'm fat, and that works to begin with, basically.

Even though your work goes on without my "intervention" through the greater part of the year, I would like to make the point that if you do play exclusively for the audience, you will suffer. Your work will suffer.

IV

It is true that in working for characterization in a role, and I don't want to dwell on it too long at this stage of your work, the imagination involves the use of certain actions and very often particularly the use of certain aspects of the body, new impulses that one gives to the body. For example, in working on Goneril, the director might tell you, "The next time you do it, she's a block of hot ice. Now work on that. Agitate your imagination around that idea. And if it doesn't work for you, we'll find some other stimulus." A notion like that would excite me very much. Or perhaps the image of a black leopard, who always excites me at the zoo. I recall with great pleasure the fact that one of the directors in the Group Theatre said about a tycoon I was playing in a play by John Howard Lawson that the man is a bulldog. So I set out to discover what "bulldog" meant to me, and I discovered it wasn't only the jaw and the teeth and the wrinkled business around the eyes, but a certain down-to-earth quality of sinking my teeth into something and not letting go until I got it. That was the bulldog quality.

The important point here is that even in grotesque or extreme cases, the characterization results from the Self, the Self within certain circumstances. The task is to free our Selves no matter whether we are playing a young man of seventeen or an old one of eighty-five.

Suppose your Action in a play is roughly "to penetrate the truth." I wish "to find out the truth." Hamlet is the supreme example. But Polonius desires to reach the truth too, doesn't he, in his way. He's always probing for it. What is the difference then between Hamlet seeking the truth and Polonius seeking the truth? What does Polonius want?

To show the world he can condense experience into aphorisms. To reveal his own cleverness.

"To reveal his own cleverness." All right, he wants to show the world how clever he is. Particularly, he wants to show the King and Queen how clever he is. Particularly to show the King. Particularly he wants to convince himself that he has an answer for everything. Yes, yes, you see, your investigation has given you a special color which would lead to characterization. Aside from the question of makeup and costume and physical helps, our problem is to show how that Action is incorporated in terms of being. How do we go about it? It's an interesting pursuit. What will be the difference between the way Polonius goes about "playing his Action," and the way Hamlet would? What can you perceive is the manner, shall we say, in which Polonius would perform his actions? What do you see? Again, I ask you to imagine yourself in the theatre, sitting where you are now in the third row, and you see a performance of *Hamlet*. What do you want of the character of Polonius? What will please you?

Well, there are certain given facts. Polonius is an old man. He has a daughter, Ophelia. He's a person of eminence in the court. Those are just the basic facts that are in the play. Now what I expect in Polonius is a person who unhesitatingly, unfalteringly goes out to give people the answers, to catch Hamlet in a revealing situation so as to be able to go back to the King and diagnose Hamlet's problem for the King, to solve it for him with the aplomb of a diplomat.

Those are all psychological clues for the playing of Polonius, correct enough, but what about the physicality of it? I'm sure, for example, I do a number of things as Falstaff that are physical adjustments to the circumstances of the "fatitude" of the man: the legs wide apart, a certain way of peering so as to get around my own bulk, I don't just look, it's a round look. I'm forced to describe it for you because I'm analyzing it, but I don't think about that on stage. I allow my belly to influence my mind, as it were.

Getting back to Polonius. You saw me play it. So what did you see?

I remember you reasoning very meticulously with your hands and getting them confused and trying to straighten them out again.

Now if I had said to myself, "I will reason very meticulously with my hands," I'd have strangled myself. But those things arise out of the inner feeling, the conception, the instinct about the character.

It seems to me you characterize a great deal from your feet. You move differently. Watching you do Falstaff, you move entirely differently, you place your feet entirely differently from the way you do. As soon as you enter, your feet take on different placement on the stage.

I recognize that feet can be important. I once knew a man, who still lives and acts in Hollywood. When I was very young, and he was somewhat older than I, I once asked him what is the secret of acting. "What do you do? What makes you a good actor?" He answered without pause, "Footwork, old boy." At the time I was mystified, but I found out that I could respect his judgment because all he meant was, I think, that his feet were comfortably in the right place all the time; therefore he was never lost. You remember the other day I said, "Place your feet significantly on the floor?" Well, I think he carried that into practice constantly. He usually played butlers, and his butler's feet were always in the right place. Things like that can be important, and for him they were very important in the matter of characterization.

Michael Chekhov used to say that the hands are the most delicate conveyer of what's happening inside, because the hands can't speak words. They can only speak in their way; and perhaps being hands, they touch on ideas, sensations, perceptions, that are not possible to convey by means of words.

Above all, I would urge you to adopt as your lifelong rule to simplify everything. Frankly, where I am disappointed in myself with my performance of Falstaff are the places I find that are over-complicated. Sometimes I discover in the midst of final rehearsals that things have simplified themselves out. This is due, I think, to the assertion, to whatever degree I can assert it, of Self. A year from now, if I were playing the same performance, I think you might find that it would be far more simple and much more effective. Right now, in the beginning stages of creating a role, one is apt to pile on everything but the kitchen stove; and that's good, in a way. But later you learn to excise, to cut away. Let the real person emerge, and you find everything becomes simplified right down to the eyes that I make such a point of, because behind the eye is the main intention, the Spine of the character.

To the extent that I can state it now, Falstaff's Spine is something like this: "I want to overcome this harsh unlovely reality by an unremitting desire to live, (he says 'give me life') by a constant desire to live richly, fully." Now that's a lot of words and for myself, if I remind myself that my Spine is simply "to live," it will induce, not only the fundamental desire for a good life, "Lads, boys, I love you all, let's make merry, let's have a play extempore, let's live!" Not only will it propel a moment like that; but it will also exemplify his actions on the battlefield when he says, in paraphrase, "to hell with that, I'm not for that. You can get killed out there," as the joke goes. Or the way he surmounts momentary impediments like being caught in a lie. He says, "That's not at all what I thought, what I saw, what I did. I have a perfectly good reason for the way I acted out there on Gadshill." And you can answer him in only one way—with laughter, because you can't really answer him. You can't top him. And his actions all come from the desire, as I say, to live, to *overcome* the harsh realities and cynicisms and death wishes, if you like, of a society that afflicts him. He creates his own world of imagination, of fantasy. I think this is probably the secret of his attractiveness to the cronies who cluster about him.

One begins by piling on the detail. Later on, the ability "to overcome" may be seen only in the eye with all its simplicity. For example, I'm not satisfied with the scene where I play the King. Why? Because what I want, what I would like (and I won't get it this trip), is to convey somehow to the audience through Action that this is a sublime joke. All right, I'm playing the joke. I'm the King, and Hal's my naughty son. I want, behind the look in the eye which says, "Harry, you disappoint me, you are not my son in so many ways" and all that, I would like the audience to perceive the twinkle of knowledge, of self-knowledge, of knowing it's all a joke. You ask me to play the king? All right,

"Shall I? Content." Here goes. "Now, Harry . . ." But how do you play this double thing, the double thing of "I know it's a joke" and "It's terrible the way you've been carrying on." The enjoyment of both things. I think one has to get so immersed in the material of the scene that eventually this will be apparent.

You may say you don't have to worry about that, it comes out anyway. To some extent it does. But I would like to do it consciously for I am jealous of my craft as an actor. And by the way, you should be too. Every one of you. When you learn something, salt it away and say, "There—that makes me that much more an actor, and it's mine, I like it, and I'm proud of it, and I'm jealous of it; and I can teach it."

That's another thing I haven't spoken about. In the short time we have together, I don't know that it is worthwhile dwelling on, but I do believe that every person who knows how to act, who knows how consciously to assemble his forces in order to act, should be able to convey it to someone else, simply and immediately much more than I have done. It forces me to constantly examine my craft to see whether it is sufficient for all answers.

I have two basic questions. First, how do you find the Spine and second, how can you get that Spine to turn you on so that everything you do radiates from it and reinforces it?

I'll answer by giving you the best example I know: that is Shylock. We normally say that Spine is represented by an active verb, don't we? Many of us have learned to be governed on stage by an active verb: to fight, to resist, to insist, a thousand active verbs. Now I have found that not always will the Spine be represented by just the verb. If I were to say in the case of Shylock, for instance, that his Spine is "to get his own back," "to resist" with the idea of getting his own back, that would not give me the full character. It would give me certainly a great deal to work with, but it wouldn't lead me to find the precise color and all the facets of his character. It wouldn't give my imagination the proper full answer. So I can tell you this story. I was reading the great speech in Shylock's first scene with Antonio, for perhaps the eighteenth time, when I was studying the part, and I daresay instinct led me to the consideration of that speech as being a root speech, one that is basically important for the whole part. If you don't know it, it goes:

Signior Antonio, many a time and oft
In the Rialto you have rated me
About my moneys and my usances:

You see what I'm doing there, by the way, something that I urge you to do in the first presentation of a soliloquy, that is, follow the simple, cerebral logic of the thing so that one knows what you are talking about. Later you can supply

all of the surrounding impulses, add the wings as it were. Remember in the last
analysis what I want of Shakespeare is flight. I said that on the first day. All
right:

> Still have I borne it with a patient shrug,
> (For sufferance is the badge of all our tribe).
> You call me misbeliever, cut-throat dog,
> And spit upon my Jewish gaberdine,
> And all for use of that which is mine own.
> Well, then, it now appears you need my help:
> Go to then, you come to me, and you say,
> 'Shylock, we would have moneys:' you say so,
> You that did void your rheum upon my beard,
> And foot me as you spurn a stranger cur
> Over your threshold, moneys is your suit.
> What should I say to you? Should I not say
> 'Hath a dog money? Is it possible
> A cur can lend three thousand ducats?' or
> Shall I bend low, and in a bondman's key
> With bated breath, and whispering humbleness,
> Say this,—
> 'Fair sir, you spit on me on Wednesday last,
> You spurn'd me such a day, another time
> You call'd me dog; and for these courtesies
> I'll lend you thus much moneys'?
>
> (I,iii)

Now it goes on, of course, but something has happened in the course of that
speech. A very interesting thing. Some detail has been repeated three times,
has been said three times. Do you know what it is? Listen. "You spit upon my
Jewish gaberdine." "You that did void your rheum (*Spitting.*)" I make it ugly on
purpose "upon my beard." "Fair sir, you spit on me on Wednesday last." (And
here I improvise by paraphrase) "I passed you on the street, and you found it
not beneath your dignity to turn aside and spit upon me, and now you come to
me for money? It is to laugh!"

Now, the fact of this spitting which is ugly, vulgar, disgusting, *disgusting*—do I
have to tell anybody here what it is like to be spat on, even if you haven't been?
If someone with full intention to insult and wound and denigrate and repress
were to deliberately and vulgarly spit on you, do I have to tell you what would
happen *inside* you? And if I said to you that this cavalier action was repeated on
an average of three or four times a week and it was something that you would
have to expect when you pulled your gaberdine about you and went out into
the streets of Venice and that throughout the year this was the kind of
behavior that you might encounter, for "sufferance is the badge of all our
tribe"; would you then begin to understand fully, tragically (I see in your faces
you do, many of you), the full burden Shylock has to carry as he pursues the

business of money lender, which is the only business allowed him? And can you then not see that this becomes the fully agitating detail that shapes and characterizes all of his actions? Can you begin to see him in his entirety? As he dresses to go out in the street, as he says goodbye to Jessica, as he goes out in the street, takes his stick and begins to walk along the street, leaving the ghetto, going outside it, huddling close to the walls when he perceives someone approaching—the Gentile, the adversary, someone, anyone. Can you not see the guarded, proud way by which he maintains his fundamental dignity as a Jew and as an individual in all of his necessary dealings with the Christians? Note that "you that did void your rheum upon my beard." The beard, the very symbol of manhood and especially important to the Jew, the Jewish beard. Can you see, filling out the picture for yourself, if not for what Shakespeare has given you to work with; how, after he has finished his job on the Rialto, he returns home, having weathered the insults and the assaults on his Jewish dignity, with the utter relief of a man who now looks forward to a peaceful evening at home with his daughter, his wife Leah being dead, how he retires and relaxes into the camaraderie of the synagogue, perhaps with his friend Tubal, how the Sabbath becomes thrice dear to him because it is a release and a relief from all that business. How then he girds his loins to put on a gaberdine on a Monday morning or whenever it is and goes out again into the streets of Venice to encounter the same routine. And all this arises, you might say, out of a few drops of saliva. I say this only because when I, in the study of Shylock, perceived that Shakespeare had put this dreadful detail in for a purpose, only then did the whole part become clear to me, the whole thing. No one had to tell me how he would behave and what he would do for the whole of the play from the moment of entrance to: "Three thousand ducats!" This comes from a representative of the people who spit on me. "Well? Who? Antonio? Well! The prime spitter of them all. And he wants it, eh? I see." Then the scene at home with Jessica—I paraphrase: "I'm leaving. For God's sake, keep the house closed. Don't let anybody near it. Take care." That peculiar burdened, constantly anxious and harried feeling that comes from someone who has "had it." All leading, of course, to the great speech, "Hath not a Jew eyes . . ." Because (as I wrote once*) the words, "Hath not a Jew eyes, hath not a Jew organs, dimensions, senses, affections, passions," and so on, tremble on his lips *when we first see him.* The man who on his first appearance has only the words,"Three thousand ducats," is the man who in the same breath, can, if he wishes, add "Hath not a Jew eyes, hath not a Jew hands," and so on. "And Antonio bound, Well?" "Hath not a Jew eyes," etc. You see what I mean. I'm drawing the line of tension between all the parts of the play, from the beginning to the end. This

---

*"On Playing the Role of Shylock" in *The Merchant of Venice* by William Shakespeare. New York: Dell Publishing Co., Inc., 1958.

will be the same man who goes to court and says, "To hell with it, if I die for it, now I am going to get a bit of my own back." Here's where the literal spine, "I'm going to get a bit of my own back," can be justified. Put more subtly and more inclusively, the real Spine has everything to do with the *fundamental conflict* of the man. And Shakespeare has given you the clue in the speech to Signior Antonio. Now you may say, "Yes, you've made it so clear for yourself that it's got to be that way for me." I don't know. If you ever come to the playing of Shylock, I hope you'll find other clues maybe, so as to examine the thing in a different light.

The whole process of rehearsal is a search for the Spine. You may never find the words for it, but I think you can find the right Spine for yourSelf. The Spine is to be found in a number of ways. You can persist in evoking it by means of an active verb, and it helps, for it's undoubtedly good to think about it that way. But I think there are other ways which are more immediately activating. There *can* be other ways. In the search for the Spine of Lear, and I won't go into it to the extent that I did with Shylock, I found a kind of double idea to support the part because *Lear* is such an immense play that it almost requires a double spine. It's like driving two horses instead of one. But both ideas are right in the script. It's always in the play. It dare not be outside the play because that would have nothing to do with the case. One of the things Lear cries out in the midst of the storm is "Pour on! I will endure." He says it to the storm, but it applies to everything that has engulfed and afflicted him. He says, in effect, "Nothing, nothing is going to overwhelm my will, my spirit, my human identity. I swear it. I swear it by all the gods. Nothing. The storm, the hatreds, the cynicism, the rottenness of the world I am surrounded with. None of this is going to ever get me down."

Now you know that is a powerful idea, a powerful Spine and what I found was that the whole play built to that and descended from it. But not only that. The other idea that agitated me was the idea that is expressed in his so-called Mad Scene when he says,

> They flattered me like a dog, and told me
> I had the white hairs in my beard ere the
> black ones were there. To say 'ay' and 'no'
> to everything that I said! 'Ay' and 'no'
> too was no good divinity. When the rain
> came to wet me once and the wind to make me
> chatter, when the thunder would not peace
> at my bidding, there I found 'em, there
> I smelt 'em out! Go to, they are not men
> o' their words: they told me I was every-
> thing; 'tis a lie—I am not ague-proof.

The peculiar sourness of that conclusion after, "They told me I was everything; 'tis a lie—I am not ague-proof" is one of the very roots of the play because what it expresses is "no man is everything." But as Lear I had wanted to be told I was everything. So the whole statement almost of the basic humanity of Lear is in that seemingly incidental phrase. Nevertheless, for me it fed the peculiar search of Lear for his own identity. Now you could have said at the beginning, the Spine of Lear is the search for one's manhood, the search for one's Selfness. That's a good spine, but I doubt if I could play it just as such: "I will search for my own identity." That's the same thing Peer Gynt does. Hamlet does that. In a sense, Juliet does. She searches for her own integrity. But it's not "juicy" enough, so to speak, to stimulate my own juices. I want my juices to be stimulated when I am playing a part—a rich part, and every part contains within itself the secrets of its own juice.

The Spine is an invitation to the imagination. It says, "Come out, come out, wherever you are." When you have a mass of turbulent, tumbling emotions, all of which wish to collide and come together and confederate in a startling and exciting account of a play which is as thrilling as *Lear* or *Hamlet* or *Henry IV*, well then, the possibilities are endless to give imagination its full play.

Very briefly, a third example I'd like to give from my own experience is Prospero in *The Tempest*. Again, with Prospero, like Shylock, you could identify his Spine as: "I want to get my own back." It certainly fits the play. And the fact that it resembles the ordinary, mechanical Spine of Shylock is not surprising in a perusal of Shakespeare's work from the beginning to end, because Shylock's pursuit of vengeance in that relatively early Shakespeare play (which is justified and fully motivated, as I've tried to show) is balanced at the very end of Shakespeare's writing career by the desire to forgive, the desire to reconcile, to harmonize. Against one is placed the other; and in between is *Lear*, in which the whole world goes to pot and is examined for its rottenness. And so we have the figure of Shylock in the beginning, Lear in the middle, and Prospero at the end. Now, during the rehearsals of *The Tempest*, I came to the scene in which I as Prospero am about to take my revenge on the visitors to the island; and Ariel, my faithful spirit, reports that my former subjects are weeping. They are in deep despair, particularly Gonzalo (whom Prospero loves). And then Ariel softly says, "If I were human—If I were human, I would forgive them." "If I were human." There's something so touching about that that it transforms not only Prospero's desire for revenge, but restores him to *his true nature*, his deepest sense of Self. He responds with the promise, "And so I shall . . . and they shall be themselves." This is the true magic of Prospero, of the play.

I can't emphasize too often that the whole process of rehearsal for the actor exists in order to find the essence of the character. I am, I suppose, by nature and inheritance a bit of a perfectionist. I recognize that that can be a danger, if one doesn't move from here to there until "here" is perfect. That's a little wasteful at times in the theatre, but I do get an image of something like "a consummation devoutly to be wished" for which I work, and I am not satisfied unless I have accomplished something close to that image. I'm a pain in the neck on this point, and I apologize to all of you who have suffered with me in rehearsal. But, you've got to dash in and bloody your nose! Make a damn fool of yourself in rehearsal, because that's where experimentation is necessary; and good direction, of course, will shuttle you into the right structure for your image.

As I told you, in my own thinking about Falstaff, for example, his whole spine is expressed in the three words, "give me life." Now in rehearsal it's the actor's job to translate it into action, in terms of himself, his own action. In the case of Falstaff, for me it comes down to enjoyment, and that's what I worked for in rehearsal. The enjoyment of being prodded awake by Hal. The enjoyment of facing the world! I love that moment where I try to pull myself out of sleep into a recognition of light and people. The enjoyment of trying to prod Hal into being a fellow conspirator—a fellow thief. The enjoyment of covering up my own guilts. The enjoyment of being recognized as "Monsieur Remorse" by Poins, who knows me better than any other character in the play, who know my ups and downs. The enjoyment of pretending, of faking, of coming into the tavern after the robbery as if I had been one of the three last survivors of the human race. The physical enjoyment of the pretended fight, of the sheer mental agility of encountering Hal with a characterization of his father. Then in the latter part of the play, which is more serious, the enjoyment of tearing the mask off that word "honor," the enjoyment of revealing to the audience his own buffoonish knavery in his confession, "I have misused the king's press damnably," of his own corruption. So here is a very large spectrum of enjoyment going all the way from corruption to mental maturity.

And in working for the Spine, don't forget that this character issued out of Shakespeare's mind, out of Shakespeare himself. In a way these characters can be considered as facets of Shakespeare's own understanding of life. His own forgiveness of life. This is what makes him so very great. So extraordinary. My wife said the other day, *there* is a man I wish God had let live. Let him write about the present day. We certainly need somebody to assess the present time in the way that Shakespeare assessed his time. This vastness and variety of colors in Shakespeare should help us as free, creating, inventing animals in the theatre to see the characters and the words and the themes in our own way. A prime example for me has always been Shylock. Shylock was probably considered in Shakespeare's time and immediately thereafter as a clown. For us, this is not possible. Not because our times are so enormously different from Shakespeare's. We still have massive prejudices. But because Shakespeare himself left a vast space all around his characters, which humanized them. In other words, he is three centuries ahead of his time. And Shylock is, I think, to be recognized and played in the light of what we in the present know about and feel about humanity, about psychology, about the simplicity of the human spirit, about the desire for a better world.

In the same way we can understand Richard the Third, not so much as a dynamic, tyrannical wheeler, a willful power, but as a sufferer, a man tormented by his crippled condition, a man whose mind is warped by the fact that it is contained in a crippled form. I doubt if this is the way Burbage played him. But Shakespeare was such a world-shaking genius that he left space for us to interpret his characters with our particular insights.

Getting back to the concept of the Spine then, I hope you will see that the essence of a character is more than just the active verb that we are taught to use by many teachers of the Stanislavsky approach. It's good, of course, for enclosing the main action of the character, but I look for something more exciting. Spine represents that stimulus which will provide the most incentives to action, to put it concisely. One of my favorite phrases in the study of acting was invented by Vakhtangov, the great Russian director, who worked with Michael Chekhov. The phrase arose between them because they were very excited about working with each other and with the characters they were examining. The phrase is "Agitation from the Essence." Agitation *from* the Essence, not *of*. It is as if a certain aspect of power were perceived and released from which would emerge every action of the character that was being played. Now the word "agitation" indicates again what I feel should take place on every stage. Agitation is not casual; it is not resigned. Even if you are required by the play to be passive, to be indifferent, even that can and should be done by the actor with agitation. To take an immediate example, the agitation that propels Falstaff, propels him, when he thinks how marvelous it is *to be alive* and that accounts for all his actions, every one of them. At times he might simply want to say "I like you. I like to be in the same room with you, you sweet son-of-a-bitch." That too comes from that agitation. Of course, all he does say to Poins is, "Thou hast damnable iteration," but "sweet son-of-a-bitch" is imbedded in that line, and his love of life and his love of Hal, as representative of young life, is all imbedded in that line. In other words, to be alive "like mad." And this really applies to all parts, all of them.

A great stimulus to this, and I can't leave without saying it, is poetry. Actors should read poetry constantly. Read it aloud. Get together and read poetry at each other. And listen to the music. And love acting.

Agitation from the essence—a marvelous phrase. To find the essence and then be agitated by it throughout, creating a unity in the part so that nothing you do is alien to it. What, for example, is the essence of Lady Hotspur? What is the phrase we remember most about her? Two phrases: One of them is, "Out, you mad-headed ape" and the other is, "I swear I'll break your little finger." This combination of physical attack—she's really "breaking" his little finger—and her utter devotion and love is what is marvelous about her. She radiates a special relationship to Hotspur that would not be the relationship, say, of the Hermione you've been working on, to her husband Leontes. Find what that essence is, so that you will be constantly upheld by it, so that it will constantly feed your fire as Lady Hotspur. That's why a boiling down of the orthodox method, in the way I have done, is of value. It can shorten the time you have to dig away. Dig! Of course, dig. Read the books. Read Stanislavsky. Read Chekhov. Read Vakhtangov. There's a helluva lot in all those books, but the key, the key, lies in the direction, I believe, of Self-Action-Object; and this is designed to shorten the time of work before you.

Just this morning I came across an article by John Ciardi. It's a kind of testimonial to another poet who died this year. It has a curious bearing on our work. I discover more and more that there are things basically true of one aspect of life or art which are basically true of others. And it invites you to believe that there is a kind of underlying "bog" which is constantly moving beneath everything we practice in art especially, and perhaps even in life. It seems to me that the relationship between all the arts leads one to say, "Why yes, that's what I think about Shakespeare! That's what I think about acting! That's what I think about music!"

Ciardi begins by saying, "A poet has no true biography outside his poems." And immediately I begin to think, yes, that's true of Shakespeare. We don't know very much about Shakespeare and the things we know are peculiarly contradictory—nothing to suggest the greatness that is represented by William Shakespeare. "A poet has no true biography outside his poems. At times the poet within that physical body moves, always in ways invisible to the biographer . . . and takes on the new non-spatial existence of a poem, a kind of existence apart from the biographical 'is' and into a formal 'as if.'

"When that motion into the 'as if' succeeds, a voice is formed, a voice always deeply related to the speaking voice of the physical identity of the poet, but always at a depth that eludes our best guesswork. When the poem is good, we have the power of its voice along with the mystery of that power."

"The power of that voice." And what is that voice in our case? I spoke about it being the secret of power of the actor. "The power of that voice." We have "the power of that voice along with the mystery of that power." And that element of mystery is something you will always stare at in amazement and never quite get. The edges of many of the plays of Shakespeare—practically all—die away. A prime example is that old mysterious play, *King Lear*. The mystery of *King Lear* is precisely what I would like to get close to capturing when I do Lear in defiance of Lear's five-fold "Never."

At any rate, Ciardi continues: "Once that voice is formed and its power and mystery are felt, critics like to assert that it is immortal. What such critics mean, of course, is that language matters, that the human race needs—in something like the way most men need religious sanctions—those moments when language seems to form into an artifact or emotional summation, and that such passages will endure as long as men can respond emotionally to the language in which that voice spoke at its moment of summary."*

*Ciardi, John, "Manner of Speaking," in *The Saturday Review*, February 21, 1970, p. 20.

What the author here is really trying to say, what he is driving at, is a very difficult thing for him to express, but the whole idea rings a bell between our work and Shakespeare's. The sense of Self, our work, which aims at identifying with this overwhelming and mysterious Object—Shakespeare. "The rest is silence."

The Theatre Guild production of *Volpone*, 1928.
L. to r.: Helen Westley, Morris Carnovsky, Sanford Meisner, McKay Morris, Alvah Bessie. Set by Lee Simonson.

The Theatre Guild production of *The Brothers Karamazov*, 1927. Lynn Fontaine and Morris Carnovsky.

The Theatre Guild production of *The Brothers Karamazov*, 1927.
L. to r.: George Gaul, Alfred Lunt, Morris Carnovsky, Edward G. Robinson.

The Theatre Guild production of *Hotel Universe*, 1930.
Morris Carnovsky, Ruth Gordon.

Imagination

Light thickens; and the crow
Makes wing to the rooky wood:
Good things of day begin to droop and drowse;
Whiles night's black agents to their preys do rouse

(*Macbeth*, III,iii)

Are we to leave the accomplishment of those lines to the lighting expert and the cameraman? Or Special Effects? Without that kind of assistance, where is the actor who can come within a mile of achieving those words, those images? The very idea of the two words, "Light thickens," is overwhelming, conveying as it does the sense of clotting evil about the figure of the assassin, Macbeth. This is no mere description of night falling, it is a sinister collaboration between Nature and Man at their most murderous. A tragic commitment from which there is no return. The moment teems with pressure and activity, as always with Shakespeare. A vertigo of imagination.

It might even be said that the protagonist of this play is not Macbeth but Imagination itself. The task, then, for the actor is unusual and startling: not only to identify with the temptation and progressive corruption of this betrayer-assassin, but to take into himself the fever which infects every moment of Macbeth's career. How is this to be done, even in contemplation? To begin with, in responding to moments such as these, the actor may experience a sensation which I can only describe as a lifting of wings—flight. Paradoxically this impulse may also be visceral, generated as it is by the actor's desire to reach, to embrace, and to incarnate the thing seen; and desire always signifies Action. Those moments must be cherished and built on. The movement I describe does not and should not take refuge in mere reflection or daydreaming; it is dynamic and therefore "muscular," it molds from within. It is this *physical* aspect of the actor's imagination which encourages me to think of it as having muscularity. Quite literally it wrestles and tangles with its Objects.

The inner state of a Macbeth, transfixed by an image connoting the accumulation of evil and producing a physical sense of pollution and smog of the spirit, tremendously compelling, is a preparation for action. The riot of imagination in this case is almost a weakness in him, considering the fact that he is after all a warrior, a soldier, who might be expected to give small compunction to the business of killing. But he does, and that's the point about Macbeth. When he stops to think, he starts to imagine; and this in a way is his undoing. It weakens him, undermines his personality. The symbol of a Lady Macbeth going mad illustrates another breakdown of the personality because of imagination, another example of how imagination as a "muscle" reaches out to extinguish her.

Imagination is rooted in experience, personal experience; and the "muscular" act of imagination consists first of all in seeing very sharply, and second, in bringing similar or dissimilar observations together into a new significance. A molding, welding action. I think of that astonishing juxtaposition in the last act of *Tristan and Isolde* when the feverish and delirious Tristan, hearing Isolde's voice, rears upward exclaiming: "Ich höre das Licht!" ("I hear the light!") The very existence of symbols, of metaphors, is born of similarities. For myself, I usually establish connection in my mind or through my actual eyes with the images that I see and then allow them to make further suggestive connections from my reservoir of personal experience. Suggestiveness, of course, is one of the products of the use of imagination; again, "this is like that." That same moment from Macbeth, for example, recalls to me one night in my childhood when I was terribly frightened by a sound and a movement I heard outside my window; I have no doubt that kind of thing embeds itself in our experience. We don't need to have murdered anybody or been subject to the dreadful nightmares of a Macbeth or Lady Macbeth, but we know what they are. It's as if they've already been outlined for us.

For the actor then, I think that one of the most precious gifts brought by an attuned imagination is the release of emotion. An image was created by Shakespeare with that intention. Perhaps the process, if it isn't grasped from Shakespeare himself, can be grasped from another poet, Keats. Consider his *Ode to the Nightingale*. What is the first impact that the poem makes on you? When you've thought about it and then return to it with the love that you've stored up for it, you will perhaps be held with the very first words, "My heart aches." Now, actually, in terms of human experience, Keats needn't have said any more than that. That's the burden of the poem: the announcement, the premise. It describes the emotional state into which he has been thrown by listening to the voice of the nightingale. But then he goes on to expand that; he explains why his heart aches. The poem begins to scintillate and coruscate in terms of images. The nightingale's song is the occasion, the release, or key to a flood of associations; and at the end it all works to the final statement: "Fled is that music:—Do I wake or sleep?", a kind of bemused condition in which the poet is left suspended. A resolution as mysterious as "The rest is silence" or the end of *King Lear*. From contemplation through imagery to conclusion the poem has *movement*; the poet, *involvement*.

Herein lies the parallel with the actor's work. The word is involvement, and it begins with the first moment in which the actor sees his character. What is he like? How does he walk? How does he bear himself? What is his face like? What kind of look is that in his eye? In the case of Shylock I summed it all up in the image of a beleaguered wolf, beset by enemies. That wolf-image actually comes out of the play, for Shylock is described in that manner by his enemies. An image like that sets you off much as Keats's explosions of image must have come from somewhere in his own profoundly felt experience.

In the same way that particular image of the wolf, relative to Shylock, initiates a storm of inner activity. That's where the actor "lives," as we say. If you did no more than assume that Shylock looks like a wolf or better still, a wolf beset by dogs, by enemies, it probably wouldn't immediately change your outer look, but inside you the image of the man-wolf would begin to form itself. Then certain effects would take place within your body, and begin to show particularly about your face and eyes, ultimately affecting your whole physical attitude. And all this is uniquely activated in response to the particularized image evoked in you by the figure of Shylock. Finally in the costume and makeup you will be able to make this transformation as visible as possible. But at the moment when you are assuming the qualities of this creature, you simply allow the central image to have full play. And in rehearsals, of course, you test it from day to day: perhaps, for example, thinking of Gratiano, that brutal jackbooted stormtrooper, as a dog baying around your heels; but by and large, when the imagination is given its impetus and is functioning with full force, substitutions such as these are not necessary. You need only respond within the given circumstances of the play and of the scene. The important thing is allowing one's whole equipment to respond freely to the stimulation from wherever it comes. It may not come from the image, but it usually does.

It's not so much imagination itself that we need to grasp, but we desire to create roads to freeing and stimulating the imagination, removing all impediments in the road to the fullest realization of the final image that we see. In general, as far as the student is concerned, it may be pointed out that this process can be developed by certain means: reading poetry, listening to music and so forth. As the sensitive nature of the young actor deepens, he begins perhaps to adopt the poet's habit of seeing the likenesses between things around him, so that he perceives not only the glory of falling in love, say, but the pathos. He perceives the opposites in life. The through-action that is prompted by the spine is not always a clear thing; like life itself, it is mixed with all kinds of transitional and warring elements. Obviously the more deeply developed the actor's imagination becomes, the deeper he will be able to explore and communicate the opposites in the role. The moment you engage yourself in playing a part, you begin to ask questions of it. "How does he express himself? What is the movement of his soul in the midst of that body? What is the nature of the body that accompanies the movements of the soul?" (I use the word "soul" because there is perhaps no better word.) It all involves what the character wants, what his high point is, what it is that stimulates him to his fullest activity—the Spine, supported by the experience of one's own life and the liberated imagination. In the playing of Shylock, there are very many subtleties that lie between the words. In his initial encounter with Antonio, the memory of former encounters with him colors that first scene. Where shall that come from but the imagination?

I am not Shylock myself, but I can sympathize with Shylock, and sympathy is the bridge by which imagination enters into the character. After all, the character lies outside of us and our endeavor is to reach it, identify with it, and eventually to incorporate it.

This act of incorporating the image does not mean imitating what I see in my mind's eye, a character that I see outside myself. What makes imitation a *final* act of creation is the admixture of the Self. If I were simply to imitate a monkey, let us say, it might be amusing enough, but it's the final merging of myself with the *idea* of monkey which makes it a creative act. It's all very amusing to see people give vocal representations of Cagney or Barbra Streisand, but they haven't really captured the soul of the person. Acting all goes back to the proper use of one's Self within the given circumstances. We return again and again to the formula of Stanislavsky: *Truth in the midst of given circumstances.* This is what the job of the actor is, and the only truth that the actor can really hope to command is *his own truth.*

One of the very interesting phenomena that happens constantly in the process of creating a part is that you are so attuned inside yourself to the need of embodying the role, that it seems almost as if everything around you collaborates in your search. It's as if you were wandering along the seashore, and the waves bring in a pebble or a shell and deposit it at your feet, and you say, "Yes, I can use that." You will see someone in the street, and you exclaim to yourself, "That's the man! That's what I want!" These gifts brought to you in that period of work are really emanations of your own imagination, because you yourself are demanding them, needing them, looking for them. Not only do images actually live outside you, but you yourself are drawing them to yourself. This is something that happened to me while I was working on Lear. I would be sitting in a hotel room looking at a nondescript rug on the floor, and suddenly I would see a face forming and looking out at me from the fabric. I would even hastily take a pad of paper and sketch what I saw, because the element of make-up is not unimportant by any means. What kind of beard shall a Lear use? What kind of eyes? What kind of wig? All these things. And suddenly you see them. The designs in wallpaper will suddenly look at me and present an image. Not a very lofty exercise of the imagination, but there it is! It happens and it's all around you. Always there's a search, and sometimes if you're lucky, random circumstances outside yourself will bring you extraordinary answers.

Of course your past experiences and observations are also waiting to be used. The whole idea of "a broken face" occurred to me in my study of Shylock. I remembered and saw in imagination a certain character I had often encountered in the streets of St. Louis in my childhood, a very pathetic, miserable, and tragic creature with whom I sympathized profoundly. There it is, the current of feeling which involves you with the character. It's almost as if you were saying: I sympathize so much with that person that I wish to be that person, I *am* that person.

Also the power which is added to you when you do a character like Shylock can sometimes come to you from unexpected sources. For example, the use of a stick. You can suddenly find that the stick, with which you go walking in the streets of Venice, is something which affirms a sense of power in you. And sometimes this happens in the last hours of rehearsal. You put your costume on, and it's like the capstone on the edifice. You have built something which lacks perhaps a final confirmation; and suddenly you see the whole thing, not only in the mirror, but you feel it in your bones. A certain pulsing quality is added which feeds itself into the unity of the character. All the facets, all the elements are in place, but there is something at the very end which is added, which is your *power*; and that again emanates from the Self. It's as if your costume and your appurtenances were all tickets of admission to your final Selfhood.

I have failed in certain parts, but I think I can say that whatever it was I was driving for was to some extent achieved simply because I had a strong image at the beginning. I don't think, for instance, that I was very successful at playing Claudius in *Hamlet*. I think I lack certain elements of the flesh, to put it bluntly, in my own make-up. I could give a good account of myself, but it wasn't the real thing. What did attract me about the possibility of doing Claudius, however, was the conflict in the man. The external appearance that he presents to the world is at war with the inner image that Claudius has of himself. This is a very important element in the character, because, as is brought out in the play, despite all the man's competence: his diplomacy, smoothness, his eroticism, and his actual love for Gertrude, he has a burning center of guilt. The actor's imagination pursues that combination: how to find the union of the outer manifestations of a Claudius with what is going on within him. So that at the end of the play, Hamlet's antagonist lies there dead, but you understand what he was all about. I had never played a statesman of that kind, a man who was involved in a fundamental act of betrayal, murder, and seduction, a betrayal of Nature which is a recurrent theme in Shakespeare. When I think of the kind of person that Gertrude would require to be her lover, her husband, and her king, a great figure of power suggests itself to me, of masculine power, diplomatic and political; and a man who is relaxed within that power. That becomes tragic when the torment he is suffering from is revealed. "Oh, my offense is rank, it smells to heaven." Those are strong words, and many actors I have seen play Claudius have said that speech very well, but they didn't altogether believe it. I don't think I gave a full account of myself in that speech, but at any rate the direction I chose was what I have here described.

The whole process of letting your mind run freely over the image that you see produces a curiously physical activity. I've sometimes even felt it while I was doing readings to an audience. I find myself almost dancing, rising and falling on my toes; though I am really doing nothing but reading. It's the presence, almost the physical presence, of *what* I am reading that stimulates me to ride, as it were, on the words. I feel certain that a poet must respond in very much the same way. I've often visualized Shakespeare sitting alone in a lamplit room as he dashes off those lines of *Macbeth* that open this chapter. I imagine him suddenly stopping, then striding across the floor and murmuring, "My God, this is terrific! My God! Where did it come from?" And then dashing back to the writing with an acceleration of physical energy, which is visible in what follows. That's what is extraordinary about Shakespeare among other things, the energy with which he discharges his images, and I think this is probably true of all poets. Consider a poet like Gerard Manley Hopkins. It might seem to someone coming to his poetry for the very first time that it makes almost no sense, because Hopkins dismisses verbs and connective tissue. He simply dashes the images at you, and in his case the accumulation of these images adds up to God. The effect it has then is of one person's ecstasy in the face of the forces of nature dominated and governed by the idea of a God. "Glory be to God for dappled things," is the first statement of his poem, "Pied Beauty." He goes on to enumerate the things for which one ought to give glory to God, ending with "Praise Him." One line: "Praise Him."

The peculiar excitement that animates the poet translates itself to the reader. The actor too has to learn to give himself willingly to these things, not to resist. Not to say, "Of course that's the poet's way of talking, it isn't mine." No, it is and must be the actor's way of talking as well. I often say to my students that if we're going to play Shakespeare, we ourselves must become poets. That doesn't mean we must write poetry, but we can develop some part of the poetic instinct. In our case I think, not having the creative power to make images, we must at least allow the images which the poet gives us to arouse and suggest. (In the last analysis are we actors not attempting to identify with Shakespeare himself?) It is a poet's activity that we crave. Where is it to come from? Basically, of course, from the actor's sensitiveness to life, as well as his sensibilities about the author's visions, objects, and images. There's where the excitement lies. The actor, face to face with these things recognizes his own excitement; something in him expands; his feet, as it were, begin to reach for the stage floor.

He wants to act.

> The lunatic, the lover, and the poet
> Are of imagination all compact:
> . . . . .
> The poet's eye, in a fine frenzy rolling,
> Doth glance from heaven to earth, from earth to heaven;
> And as imagination bodies forth
> The forms of things unknown, the poet's pen
> Turns them to shapes, and gives to airy nothing
> A local habitation and a name.

That's Shakespeare, speaking through the mouth of that sensitive gentleman Theseus in *A Midsummer Night's Dream*. I've always wanted to substitute (sotto voce) for the word "poet" the word "actor". With a certain amount of justification, since Shakespeare himself was also an actor; and it may be that much of his verbal and image-making power stemmed from certain moments of profoundest realization on the stage. A word is a very suggestive thing. It never comes unaccompanied. It's always followed and surrounded by associations—always. Even the most basic words. A simple connective word like "but". In the most direct possible way doesn't it say "so far and no farther?" And "if"; it has the whole world of possibilities trailing after it. We perceive that after Keats set down "My heart aches" and then proceeded to elaborate the reason for the ache in his heart and images began to occur to him, he must have returned to that line again and again, discarded, altered, and rearranged the poem until it achieved perfection—always dominated by the central idea—"Because of the song of this nightingale, My heart aches, and my imagination is aroused."

The actor is commonly given grudging credit as an interpretative artist, but his function is very close to that of the original creator. It occurs to me, again and again, that all arts are fundamentally the same in the way they happen, only the manner in which they are expressed depends upon the individual and the medium he has chosen. The music of a Beethoven, a Mozart,.a Chopin, or a Stravinsky is completely distinguishable from that of any other composer and represents his fundamental—here's where we touch on the actor's province—his fundamental response to life. We take from life and we give forth in terms of art. No artist of any description can deny that. Everything coming out of life to us is transfigured or transformed in the melting pot of our individual imagination, then goes forth in another form, an arranged and significant form. We actors do the same thing. We're given the material to work with; we don't create it out of whole cloth. The material itself excites us. To the degree and in what form it excites you lies either your success or failure. You face a play by Shakespeare and it faces you, as if to say, "Here I am, put me on the stage. Make me come to life." Tremendous challenge! And you don't rise to it merely by studying the lines and putting the emphasis in the right places, but by mingling imaginatively with the whole life of the play.

I don't see acting as a second rate art. I regard it as a very beautiful and natural craft which becomes an art when it gives us those "thoughts beyond the reaches of our souls" because that's the function of all imagination.

Now it's true that the whole actor's destiny is a very transitory one—when he goes, his performances are gone; but in the striving to achieve and incorporate that final image which contains so much suggestiveness within it, his craft is very similar to that of the painter and of the composer. But despite that transitory nature there is the chance that someone may be able to say of an actor's work, "There it stands. For its time and for its quality it is unsurpassable. It is classic." I'm not even sure that the actor can recognize that quality in himself after completing a performance. I know in my own case when I play a summer of performances of Lear, keeping track of the performances which have the greatest unity and fidelity to the concept, they can be numbered on less than the fingers of one hand. Here and there you hit it in a way you like and enjoy, about which you might be able to say, "That was good," because you recognize this sudden lift of the imagination. A few years ago I saw Nancy Wickwire play Hermione in *The Winter's Tale*. That performance shared with poetry the high level of expressiveness. I'll never forget her appeal to the judges in that play—heartbreaking. As a matter of fact it provided me with a new knowledge of what that part was all about, so that I found myself sitting there and saying, "Yes, yes."

I return then to that sensation which I describe as a lifting of wings—flight. Call it what you will—"the desire of the moth for the star." I cannot resist quoting Keats again:

> Away! away! for I will fly to thee,
>   Not charioted by Bacchus and his pards,
> But on the viewless wings of Poesy
>   Though the dull brain perplexes and retards;

There it is—the lift of the imagination to overcome the drag of clay, and that loneliness in which a poet strives to create. The actor, too. He is alone with Malvolio, alone with Feste. He is alone with Lear, alone with Claudius, Shylock. Together with the poet he aspires to shape his craft in the direction of art.

Golden Boy, 1947.
L. to r.: Morris Carnovsky and John Garfield.

The Group Theatre production of *Johnny Johnson*, 1936.
L. to r.: Kate Allen, Morris Carnovsky, Phoebe Brand,
Grover Burgess, Russell Collins.
Set by Donald Oenslager.

Facing page, top: The Group Theatre production of *Golden Boy*, 1947.
L. to r.: Phoebe Brand, Morris Carnovsky, Frances Farmer.

Facing page, bottom: The Group Theatre production of *Golden Boy*, 1947.
L. to r.: Morris Carnovsky, Phoebe Brand, John Garfield, and Lee J. Cobb.

Action

For here lies the point, if I drown myself wittingly, it argues an act, and an act hath
three branches, it is to act, to do, and to perform . . .

(*Hamlet*, V,i)

The Gravedigger, in struggling to precisely define the self-evident, expresses himself in delightful redundancy. But allow me a whim: it may just
be that an Actor (always a possibility with Shakespeare) lurks behind the
transparent subtleties of the Gravedigger, and it is *he* that attempts to fix the
name of Action. The "definement" of it may not be that self-evident.

Action. Some prefer to call Action, as we use the term, "intention."
Perhaps that is an easier way of understanding it, but I believe that the
whole transaction between the Self and the Object is more intense than the
idea of "intention" suggests. Basically I feel that the quality of Action is *in its
essence* violent: sharp, energetic, and not to be denied, a struggle.

Now there is sometimes a confusion between "Action" and "activity." Action has to do with fundamental desire. Desire can be an abstract thing, but
activity is not abstract. Activity is concrete; generally I think of activity as
being the instrument of desire.

An example. Look at Peter Quince in *A Midsummer Night's Dream*. His is a
very touching and delicate desire. As producer of his little play, *Pyramus and
Thisbe*, he wants to present the most beautiful wedding gift that he can for
Theseus and Hippolyta. This is something which comes from his heart, and
it transfigures everything that he does. What he does then is expressed in the
activities of a dedicated and humble prompter. He follows the script very
closely; he corrects the actors when they go wrong; he combats Bottom's in-
flated ambitions; he even brings props along to the rehearsal in the wood.
The underlying Action (or intention) may issue in specific characterization.
It influences Quince's walk, his eyes; the actor may choose to be a trifle near-

sighted. He may use his hands in a certain way, pointing out that such and such is wrong, and such and such is right. And all these smaller choices are transfigured by the fundamental desire: to please Theseus and Hippolyta. Out of this desire is born the Action which is: to create something beautiful for them.

And the activity, then, consists of all the ways it must, of necessity, express itself. When I played the part, I had a little three-legged stool which I brought on into the rehearsal in the woods, because it was necessary for me, as a prompter, to have something to sit on with my script. Then, when Bottom disappeared into the brake and reappeared with the ass's head on his shoulders, I used the three-legged stool to ward him off, to protect myself in case he became violent. That emerged from the simple necessity of dealing with crises when they occurred; and usually they occurred with regard to Bottom. Bottom impels them, but underlying every such crisis is the quality of Quince's fundamental desire.

The violence that I attribute to the quality of Action is pretty well hidden in the case of Quince because Quince is very gentle and bookish. Driven to assert himself he can be strong in small circumstances, as when he opposes Bottom's desire to play everything. That is a simple example of Action resulting in activity. It seems so simple that it would almost be taken for granted, but actually it is a small example of what can take place on a large scale.

In the case of Shylock, one might simply accept the Action abstractly stated as "to get my own back" or "to take revenge on the Christian world that oppresses me." But this statement of the Action, which is fairly violent, doesn't really happen until the play is pretty well advanced: until his house has been violated, until he has been robbed, and his daughter stolen from him. Then it asserts itself completely. What, then, is the prevailing Action (desire) which *precedes* this particular Action? My own choice reveals Shylock's attitude as expressed in his words to Antonio:

> I would be friends with you, and have your love,
> Forget the shames that you have stain'd me with,
> Supply your present wants, and take no doit
> Of usance for my moneys,

(I,iii)

To me it is a highly important statement, and I take it literally with no overtones of hypocrisy; for it expresses not only Shylock's desire, but in a basic sense the desire of all men. Who wants to enter into the jungle of human hatred and prejudices without making some effort to clear a path through it? I don't say that this is Shylock's overall Action. That Action gets changed when the crisis comes; and after that, there is no question about what he wants. But fundamentally all the disappointment, all the hatred and the desire for revenge, all that happens in the latter part of the play comes with stronger force because it was preceded by the desire to set things right with his inveterate enemy: "Why can't we get along, you and I?" So I would say Shylock's fundamental Action has to do with a final effort to try and reconcile things between himself and Antonio. After the crisis, however, another Action takes over—"to finally have it out with this stupid, vulgar, hateful prejudice by recourse to the law."

It would be difficult to subsume all of this into some vague statement of the action such as "to set things right" because of the startling things that inevitably dominate our thinking about the character, for example the fact that he actually brings a knife and scales into the courtroom to exact his justice. This is what we incline to remember when we think of Shylock. But for a fuller view of the character, we should start with the portrait of a man who lives in a terribly difficult world and who makes a last effort to reconcile it to himself; then, when he's frustrated, he takes a different road. So you might say his line of Action is suddenly derailed. I know many people won't agree with that. It used to be thought that the first scene with Antonio should be played with a very obvious desire to defeat Antonio, "to get him in a spot"; but I prefer to think that Shylock wants to nail him down, to say "Look! Look at the impossibility, look at the stupidity of your attitude toward me. Look at the contradiction of your spitting on me, insulting and defiling me in the street publicly and cowardly, since I have no way of fighting back; and now coming to me, of all people, and asking for money. Isn't it ridiculous? Isn't the recognition of this stupidity the reason why we, why all people ought to get together?"

I would be friends with you, and have your love . . .

But when it comes to making the bond, there's the difficulty for the actor. An actor working from the traditional interpretation might say, "Well, there it is in a nutshell. He makes a bond which involves the cutting of a pound of flesh from a human being. This proves that he is basically vengeful. It's horrible!" I must admit, from the point of view of the literature of villainy, that makes a very interesting picture, but it is not so. It seems to me that the only way the statement "I would be friends with you" can be reconciled with the great scene later when he indicts all Christians with inhumanity ("Hath not a Jew eyes") is through some such interpretation as I suggest.

Furthermore, in my own playing of the role I took Shylock's resorting to the bond with Antonio as a joke, a sinister joke, that occurs to him *in mid-passage.*

> Go with me to a notary, seal me there
> Your single bond; and in a merry sport,
> If you repay me not on such a day,
> In such a place, such sum or sums as are
> Express'd in the condition, let the forfeit
> Be nominated for an equal pound
> Of your fair flesh . . .
>
> (I,iii)

Now, *your fair flesh* could be interpreted as: "You think it's so much fairer than my flesh." I choose not to look at it that way. For me the turning point is right in the middle of the speech:

Go with me to a notary, seal me there
Your single bond; and . . .

There at this very point comes the break. When I came to this moment, I took a long pause as the idea occurred to me. The motivation?—in paraphrase:

"I'm not going to let you off without some sort of agreement. After all, between people involved in business there's got to be an understanding, a bond. But what shall be the nature of the bond? I've just been talking about money, about *taking no doit of usance for my moneys*; and I'm going to stick to that, but a bond we must have, and we'll write it down. What shall it be?"

And suddenly a grisly joke occurs to him.

And . . . Pause. "I've got it."

. . . in a merry sport,
If you repay me not . . .

"And you know of course I'm joking because who would propose such an impossible thing?"

If you repay me not on such a day,
In such a place, such sum or sums as are
Express'd in the condition, let the forfeit
Be nominated for . . .

"What?"

. . . an equal pound
Of your fair flesh to be cut off and taken
In what part of your body pleaseth me.

And it's a joke. Which, by the way, Antonio receives as a joke.

Content, i'faith: I'll seal to such a bond,

For of course he's certain in his mind that his argosies are going to come in safely, and he'll be released from the bond.

Bassanio, on the other hand, is outraged and shocked by this suggestion. It's only later, when events propelled by the callous adversaries of Shylock—the robbery, virtually the rape of Jessica, that the joke becomes grim fact; and Shylock determines: "All right. I happen to have this paper, which by law entitles me to this, and I'm going to see it through. You've taken my flesh; now, I'll get yours."

The Action of the initial scene for Shylock is simply to get Antonio to enter into some kind of agreement which at least has the shadow of amicability. The end of the scene finds Shylock saying,

> Then meet me forthwith at the notary's;
> Give him direction for this merry bond;
> And I will go and purse the ducats straight;

Shylock thinks that at long last he's made some sort of connection with Antonio.

Now I'm sure that many an actor will dismiss this whole idea. I find that it works and that it's justified in the play. I worry about whether this point gets over, whether that pause that I've mentioned is justified, but as I think about it, abstractly even, I think it is. It's a perilous choice. But in this respect I go along with Harold C. Goddard* who maintains basically that the actions of man revolve around good and evil and that the natural bent of humanity is rather toward good than evil. When you search for the good aspects of what seems to be an out-and-out villain, you are attempting to discover the fuller dimensions of the character. As in Richard the Third's case. What makes him so attractive in so many ways, sympathetic even? Can it be the fact that he too is distorted and contorted by nature, and all his life he's had to overcome this distortion which has reflected itself in his mind as well as his body?

When I refer to Action linking Self and Object, as I do, I intend the word a little bit differently than it is normally used. We agree that Action represents the desire of the character, but I think my favorite Italian word "rimbombare" comes into play here, the kind of perpetual stimulation that takes place if an actor realizes his given circumstances in a play and proceeds to respond to them. I must again refer to the role of Shylock which is a classical example for me because I learned so much by doing it. Consider his first encounter with Bassanio in the light of all the given circumstances which we've discussed: the very act of going out into the Rialto to do business being fraught with conflict. He knows Bassanio only vaguely; perhaps through reference to Antonio, who is his main enemy. And immediately the Object, Bassanio, stimulates Shylock to remember all the wrongs he has suffered at the hands of his natural opponents, the Gentiles in the play.

Bassanio asks him for the loan; and here let me attempt to suggest the inner dialogue of an actor's mind—transitional, continuously alive.

"A loan? He, the friend of Antonio asks me for a loan? I'm not simply going to say yes or no. I'll consider it."

After the moment of deliberation that ensues he has his first line:

Three thousand ducats. "That's a lot of money." *Well.* "Continue. Tell me under what circumstances I should accede to your request." A final study of this man who is, as he knows, the emissary of Antonio, his understudy so to speak, Shylock continues,

*Goddard, Harold C., *The Meaning of Shakespeare.* Chicago, Illinois: The University of Chicago Press, 1951.

For three months. "That's how long you want it for, eh? Well, go on, carry on." *Well.* "Where's the assurance that I may have that you'll pay me back?"

Bassanio answers, *For the which Antonio*—"that powerful man, that rich man"—*shall be bound.* "He's in back of me in my request."

"Oh-ho, now we come to it." *Antonio shall become bound.* "I get it." Now he nails down the connection.

But he avoids the immediate answer,—Note that all this is fraught with Action generated by the Object—when he says,

Antonio is a good man. The word "good" is very ironical, of course. He intends it to be a financial term, he's "good for the money," but of course the overtone is "this great and good man that you worship." And Bassanio asks, *Have you heard any imputation to the contrary? No, no, no,* he dismisses it.

This is an element of the wily and devious Shylock who arrives at the point he is driving at by roundabout methods.

My meaning, he says, "to you who seem to be a little bit dense," *my meaning in saying he is a good man is . . . that he is sufficient.* "That's all, that's all I meant, just that."

And so the scene continues with a play off the Object constantly, this handsome and rather stupid figure who confronts me, Shylock, with a request which is unusual and which I'm considering.

Now when Antonio appears on the scene, Shylock thinks, "Ah, here he is, the source, the fountainhead of this request. This is all a put-up job; and now he's here, ready to back up his young friend. He didn't want to come to me in person, because that would be beneath his dignity. But here he is."

I conceive that underneath everything and behind everything is Shylock's desire for a better world. From that, there is the corollary "if I can't get it by fair means, I'll have to get it by foul," generating the latter part of the play, "getting his own back." I am, of course, analyzing his Action from the point of view of my own interpretation, which can be differed with; but Action is always definable by the desire which is behind it and is stimulated by that "bounce" between a fully understood Object and the free and relaxed Self.

Some teachers suggest the young actor write a detailed breakdown of his role, identifying the Actions for each shift of meaning or even for each line. Analysis with me stops short at a certain point. I once had a girl and boy doing a short scene from Anouilh's *Medea* in one of my classes. They weren't up to playing the parts. They were inclined to take it very mildly, the confrontation between Medea and Jason. I pointed out the extreme violence of the Action there; and they understood and accepted it. It didn't have to be analyzed over much. I simply had them play the Action headlong, and they caught fire from the sheer excitement of doing it without analysis. In my own experience I'm not so much in favor of nailing down the proper name for an Action. It seems to me after a little conversation between director and actor the aims of any character will be simply understood.

In *Awake and Sing*, for example, Harold Clurman, our director, made the play very clear to us, so it was really a very simple process to find what you stood for, what you were. Moe Axelrod was a man who was looking for a home. He's been injured by life and fought back in his own ways by going in for petty racketeering and so on,—but nevertheless he was looking for some kind of peace and contentment, and he finds it eventually through the girl, Hennie. Young Ralph is like a Samson in chains. He's the future generation who wants to shake off the triviality and insignificance of his life in the Bronx and make the world and life possible by means of his own free actions. Jacob, the character I played, was restricted by his age. I could no longer hope to do the things that Ralphie wants to do, but I can encourage his dreams. I can *show him the right way*. I can, as a matter of fact, keep a kind of tie to the world of the future by my books and my phonograph records. The irony of his position is, as Ralph discloses in the last act after the man's death, that he hasn't cut the pages of many of the books. But there they are; they're symbols of a kind of beautiful possibility that lies in life which is unexplored. And Jacob's desire in life is constantly to point out that *there is a way* out of this mess, this filth of our daily lives.

By the way, the overall Action in that case is not unrelieved. It's not a constant grinding away. That would be very dull playwriting because it would reveal the characters as only two dimensional. There's plenty of humor and anger in Jacob. He is a human being. Although his main desire hinges upon the young people in the house, there must be room to expand out of that for the sake of the fuller Self we're always talking about; so that if new things are discovered in the course of rehearsal or even in the course of performance, provided they don't violate the fundamental aim of the play, that's perfectly good. They indicate that the creative aspect of the actor is still alive and bubbling.

In *A Midsummer Night's Dream*, the thing that propelled me as Quince was that I wanted to incorporate the image I had of him. I loved him. He was to me a darling character, and I wanted to be like that. Now what would such a character do in all the circumstances he's faced with? He too, like Jacob, wanted to point the right way. Out of this there emerges a succession of details which adds up to make a figure whose every Action naturally radiates from his Spine or central Objective. In an instance like that you almost don't have to state the Action. It states itself. It comes right out of what he does. Of course, Quince is not Jacob. The given circumstances of Jacob are the Bronx with all its difficulties and stupidities; and Quince's given circumstances are the fact that although he's a carpenter, he is perhaps the lonely intellectual in the midst of his little crew, also the fact that he's acknowledged as a leader because maybe he once did a performance of *Gorboduc* that everybody admired.

Stanislavsky has suggested that understanding one's Actions in a role is useful in order for the actor to command the "inspiration" of his performance. Speaking for myself, the only thing that will enable me to repeat a performance and arrive in general at the same results is the melting, so to speak, of the qualities of the part into myself, the act of making it my own, me. Stanislavsky said the character is seated in yourself. Michael Chekhov takes the opposite point of view. To create the character by whatever means and then to seat the Self within the character.

When I am engaged in a search for the Spine, I gather the fruit where it falls. I listen to everything that comes my way. If I can't use it, I reject it. If I can use it, I put it in my mental storehouse, and eventually it may contribute to the life of the play. But I have also found that a profusion of detail will hamper the freedom of the Self. If an actor is any actor at all, his general sensitiveness can be relied on and he will avail himself of the richness of the given circumstances surrounding him, so that he will respond in practically every case in the way the director has outlined or the play demands. I think that it is dangerous for the young actor to burden himself with moment to moment notes that he busily writes down in his script and attempts in strictest honesty to give to the director in rehearsal. One always finds actors who remind the director, "but you said . . ." Well, the director has the right to change his mind too; and he mustn't necessarily be held to the fact that he said something a week ago that he's changed his mind about. This is part of the living structuring of the play. I remember Robert Lewis (while directing *An Enemy of the People*) saying, "Don't blame me if I change my mind, I'll do it constantly." I am sure that he must have heard this "but you said . . ." again and again.

For me one of the clearest examples of the workings of this thing we call Action occurred in Jean Anouilh's *Antigone* in which I played Creon. Basically the structure of that play is simple enough. We all know the story. Antigone deliberately disobeys the law by attempting to bury her brother, and the great confrontation in the play is, of course, between her and Creon, who is head of State. Creon encounters a young woman with an iron determination to change the world, or at any rate to change the world in which she must live. Her insistence on the laws of ordinary human decency come up against a frigid, iron-bound conception of legality as represented by Creon. Creon, however, is not presented as a cold, tyrannical, mechanical figure. He has plenty of humanity; and he sets about trying to change Antigone whom, in a fashion, he loves; whom in fact his son wants to marry. So behind everything in his encounter with her is the Action, the desire, the intention of "I'm going to teach her a lesson she won't forget. I am going to show her the truth. She labors under certain misconceptions about her brothers. I am going to make her see the travesty for which she's willing to give up her life. It has become a matter of life and death. I cannot go back on my character's function as a ruler. I must win this battle, because I represent the law. I represent the State. If I allow the rumor of this disobedience to get around, I might as well resign the throne."

The moment I read the play I recognized that my over-all objective as Creon was to hold the State together. That's my function. Within that, an incident occurs (the attempted burial) which is complicated by the fact that I'm related to its perpetrator, that I *care* for her. I care about her relationship to me, to my wife, to my son; and nevertheless I am forced, by the higher power of the "Super objective," if you like, to teach her this lesson, to insist that she does what I demand.

Now one of the things that stimulated me about the role was the sheer actor's pleasure of revealing the truth. "Here it is, look at it." Creon does this in that long, long speech about the brothers. This became almost the ballast of the whole part. So that at the very beginning I knew that I was bound for that point in the text at which I would uncover the naked truth about Antigone's brothers, come what may. And the consequences do come, so that I, in my fashion, propel the play to its crisis. I encounter the girl's antagonism in the fullest form; and I am forced to pronounce the sentence of death upon her against my will. In doing that I simply obey my necessity as a character. I leave it to the audience to draw its own conclusions as to whether I am a fascist or a tyrant. In my own thinking as Creon I'm not a fascist. I am simply maintaining the world of order so that life may continue in this kingdom. I have inherited a lot of conflict and political stupidity which I intend to correct.

I sympathize with Creon. I take on his burden, so to speak. I say, "Yes, I'm right. From my point of view I'm absolutely right. My actions lead to death and a kind of momentary chaos: my wife hangs herself; my son walls himself up and dies with Antigone; and I am left with a tragic realization that perhaps law and order are not the most important things in the world, or that we have not yet found a way to cope with life." Life—which Antigone worships. Her desire to bury her brother properly represents a simple, natural, noble way of looking at life; there are certain things you don't do, you cannot do, if you are a human being. Creon says there are certain things you *must* do if you are going to be a ruler. And these are two antagonistic points of view. Creon is left, as I say, with a tragic realization, but "Let's get on with it," he says. "When is the next meeting of the Council? I must rule and I know no other way."

The reason I discuss Creon and the whole process of composing him is that almost at the first reading all these things were there. They may have been shadowy, but they appeared. An actor doesn't always have to be reminded of the realities by which he functions. He understands the nature of the conflict and the moment-to-moment nature of what he's looking at, of what his eyes and the eyes of his mind encounter. As Creon I didn't have to be told what my psychological relationship to Antigone was, and that's the main relationship in the play.

Another relationship in the play in which the Actions almost take care of themselves is my encounter with the soldier who brings me the news of Antigone's act. As an actor I enjoyed that encounter and my easy assumption of power over the soldier. That particular scene is a good example of how clearly the Action asserts itself in the give and take between Self and Object. As far as Creon is concerned, that soldier is a tool, an instrument. He's nothing. All I demand of him is the truth. "Tell me exactly what happened. Never mind all the grovelling and the explaining. I don't care about that. Who's responsible? Because I'm going to have your life, if you're responsible for this thing. You are the representative of my law, and I intend that you shall act as such." I can even feel it now as I speak: the sharpening, the sternness, which is mine as an actor and available to me anytime, is *fed* by this stupid representative of the lower classes. Once all the given circumstances in a play or in a scene are revealed and understood, the Self must be encouraged to be free. "Respond to all the elements that are available to you in this scene. There are numberless smaller ones that suggest themselves," the director might say. For example, in *Antigone*, I was greatly moved by the way Maria Tucci, who played Antigone, looked. She broke my heart. And yet I had to pronounce sentence on her. I loved her, and I had to hate her. I had to kill her. This is a subordinate value. I don't know whether this is embedded in the play, or whether it came out of me. It so happens that I like Maria very much, and this intensified the struggle and gave it more depth. I admired Antigone's integrity, her fortitude, and her humanity. At the same time I was utterly convinced that she was totally wrong; and these are the things that come out of the rebounding, that bouncing quality between Self and Object.

But finally my will must be enforced; my Action becomes the final determinant of my conduct. Creon to that extent is a tragic figure: that is, one who cannot do otherwise than respond to his fundamental necessity in the spectrum between love and hate, between power and rebellion. And there's the violence that we discussed at the beginning, not naked, but tempered by the circumstances of the play. Creon is a gentleman. He likes books; he likes antiques. All these things feed my sense of Self. He has this little boy with him, who is another aspect of his own tenderness. He is a man who cares deeply; but in the face of his profoundest necessity he *cannot do otherwise*. He is himself a tragic figure.

Counterattack, directed by Margaret Webster, 1943.
Top to bottom: Morris Carnovsky, Barbara O'Neil, Sam Wanamaker.

The Actors' Lab production of
The Inspector General, directed by
Michael Chekhov, ca. 1949.

The Life of Emile Zola, a 1937 film.

The World of Sholom Aleichem, 1953. L. to r.: Phoebe Brand, Will Lee, Jack Gilford, Morris Carnovsky, Sarah Cunningham, Jack Banning. Back to camera: Marjorie Nelson.

The Self

Sense of Self seems to be at one and the same time such an all-embracing concept, having to do with the actor's uniqueness and his very reason for creative work, as well as the very basic idea of a feeling of ease. Could you begin by distinguishing between simple relaxation and what you mean by sense of Self?

Relaxation, as I've stressed elsewhere, is the quality which removes all impediments to action. Relaxation is the *aura* within which the individual Self can declare itself and expand. This may strike the ear as perilously mystical; and that's why I am very careful to tell students not to regard the sense of Self as some kind of psychological key to the Universe, especially the universe of acting. It isn't so. It's a simple, accepting use of your own simplest and most relaxed faculties. In my own practice I have invited this condition, perhaps early in the morning when the affairs of the day haven't quite taken a tenser bent—in the bathroom shaving, as I explained in the lectures, or putting on my shoes—simple activities like that, where the necessity for utilizing time, pushing ahead in life, is removed. For the moment, all you are doing is pulling yourself together. What I noticed in myself was a desirable, carefree state. I'm smiling to myself now for putting it in such a cautious, complicated way. But I'm very concerned that the whole notion of Self should be accepted easily, and not worked for as if it were some kind of deeply buried treasure that the student has to mine out of himself by force. No, it's there, waiting to be used. And since this condition is so liberating, how desirable it would be if one could incorporate this feeling of freedom into everything one does on the stage. Because the whole condition of the stage is one of tension. The presence of the audience, the very necessity of being in certain places at certain times, the give and take of acting, the act of connection, all incline one to tension; and the whole trick, you might say, of acting is to remove these "malign" influences. What is left then will be one's Self, animated and directed by the work of rehearsals, so that at the end, as with the sculptor all the outside, the "impediments" will have been chipped away, leaving the desired image free to be itself. The more you understand about the use of your simple, unalloyed Self, the more willing and the more ready you will be to use it at the very start of rehearsals instead of waiting for it to come in the course of working on a play.

I know that in our early days as actors, we were always conscious of the listeners. Whether we admitted it or not, we wanted to please our director or the Board of Directors, whoever it might be that was out there, and our fellow actors. This is putting the cart before the horse. Sometimes you would give an effective first reading, but then you'd have to undo that in the subsequent rehearsals and work back to the truth, since that's what you were looking for. Sometimes an effective reading was all that was required. In the old days, it used to distress me very much to see certain actors—usually, I have to say, they weren't terribly good actors—read a line and then send this covert glance to the director as if to say "Did you like what I did then? Did I do it right? Was I on the right track?" after every line, after every speech. They'd say something, and then immediately this timid look would appear on their faces.

Your actor who keeps looking at the director is one of those unfortunate people whom I described in the lectures and of whom I was one at the time when I was first going job hunting in New York. I used to look at these people in the casting offices and observe their behavior, realizing that my own was not much better, though I knew that I wanted something different. I would say to myself, perhaps not consciously at first, they are not serving themselves very well, and I'm not serving myself very well. At any rate, I felt it as a kind of outrage that anyone in command had the power to do this to me. They didn't want to, perhaps; and that's precisely the point. What they were looking for were human beings, but these starched automata presenting themselves for inspection were the opposite of human beings.

Somewhere in my unconscious, I determined that that was not for me; that was not for any actor, for any person. That no one has the right to invade your Selfhood. It was a kind of declaration of independence, a tentative reaching out to the possibility of controlling that very Self, which eventually I have learned to do. I'm not always successful, mind you, but I try; I know how. So, as I said before, the first thing to do is to recognize it, and that involves saying to yourself, "I am different from *any other* person on Earth." And that recognition automatically has its rights. Then, the second phase, to accept it; and the third, to proceed to use it with all of its growing richness and power. That's how the idea of Self was born in my own experience, and how I think it exists in order to help other actors if they will realize it.

Now getting back to that rehearsal process: the initial reading of a play is vitally important; for what happens there may be the first act of connection between one's Self and the Self of the other actors. You shouldn't try to characterize over-much in the first reading. You should simply try to get that connection with the other actors, to enjoy the lines you're saying, the thoughts you're uttering; at the same time, however, not curbing yourself if you choose to act with full energy. But all along, right from the beginning, there's a test of the truth which goes on inside the actor, from the very first line. If the actor is truly aware of his Self, it is not too early, in the very same rehearsal, to say to oneself, "Look, I am *I*, and no one else; you are *you*. I respond to you as I hope you are responding to me." This certifies the trans-action between my Self and the Object, the Object and my Self.

How do you recognize that truth in yourself? Or will you just know when it's there?

You have to know, certainly. I'm thinking of a certain actress, (call her Madame X) who's loaded with talent, but who, to my way of thinking, never attained what she should have attained because she substituted a combination of charm and seductiveness and power, which she felt she must have as an actress, for the simple truth. It was a constant alloy: it stained everything she did. Very regrettable, because, as I say, she had a lot of talent, but she could not give up this *notion* of herself. It was a kind of screen which she could not possibly live without. I always had the impression that she would feel exposed if she were required to be really her Self. She came near it, for as I say, she was a good actress; but the real, special, individual Self-quality in her never was allowed to exhibit itself—never. So there you had this charm, seductiveness, sexy kind of indication, which became rather questionable after you saw it on many different occasions.

Now, of course, on Broadway, in the old star system, when I first arrived in New York, you'd have flashy stars, usually women, sometimes men. The men were great in the "character line," people like Otis Skinner, David Warfield, and the marvelous juicy, thick acting that was the hallmark of the Yiddish Art Theatre—wonderful! Those flashy men and women had brought these qualities of theirs, these seductive qualities, to a science. They were good at what they did. You didn't altogether believe in their humanity, but they were wonderful workmen. "Madame X" was a case of someone who knew better, who should have known how to release her Self and use it, but never did.

One can have the realization of how necessary a sense of truth is, and at the same time, not be capable of accepting it. It's like driving two horses that are going in opposite directions. But I think the simplest recognition of the truth in you comes from, I must repeat, again and again, the response to the Object. When you know your eyes are "colliding" with, are meeting an obstruction called Object, there's only one way to relate to it, and that is to look at it, then listen to it, and perhaps to look at it again, then to speak to it, and to be attentive to any vibrations that emanate from it, so that if suddenly, say, you are involved in a scene of anger, *you* will become involved in that same anger by your own response; but your response will always be truthful, simple and truthful.

And it works backwards as well. If you lose it, as actors sometimes do on stage, you can always refresh yourself at the source, which is the Object; and then test the other source, which is Yourself; and then go on to serve the activity of the confrontation between the two. Is that clear?

Yes, yes, I think so.

You can make the point in many different aspects of acting, but it always comes back to the fundamental set of elements—

Self, Action, and Object?

Yes. If you think I'm riding this too hard, let me say in a big parenthesis, that I'm conscious of the fact that the study of acting extends infinitely in all directions: the necessity of the actor to be a cultured person: to be at home with music, ideas, novels, and to recognize how character exists in other arts besides his own. The necessity of being a person, behind everything that he does. And then, of course, the necessity for studying the simple aspects of acting: such as the act of concentration, the act of listening, the whole business of communication, in fact, all the chapter headings of *An Actor Prepares* and *Building a Character* by Stanislavsky. All that is necessary to absorb. It's only because I insist on that that I would have the temerity to say that it can all be reduced to the unit of the Moment, which consists of our three elements. But it has to be understood by the actor, especially the young actor. It's an unending study which is tested every time he steps on stage.

I don't know if you are familiar with Grotowski's concept of the "via Negativa."

No.

His whole idea is that what one must do in training and in working on a play is to strip away as many of the hang-ups that one has as an actor and get down to the negative way, to the essence, almost the archetypal essence, of the human being. Is that the same idea as your idea of Self? Is it a stripping away of hang-ups?

Well, it sounds very close to it, yes. In the pursuit of ways of using the Self you are always making new discoveries. I ask a class to begin to try to find it by relaxing their faces, and especially their eyes; and I've noted both in myself and in them that you can push that exercise further and further. It seems limitless, the relaxation that you can induce in your eye. It is a sign that the Self is being released. It begins, I repeat, with the simple act of relaxing over which the mind has sovereignty. After all, it's the Will that propels you on the stage, and one of the uses of the Will is to command those impediments or "hang-ups," as you call them, to leave your body, to leave you free.

Perhaps this is that "negative way" that Grotowski is talking about, I'm not sure; everyone finds Self in his own way.

Just recently, about a week and a half ago, as Prospero, which is an intermittently quiet enough part to provide me with moments of solitude on the stage, I was free to make mental comments on my performance and on the play, or whatever commanded my attention. This double life needn't surprise you because it's constantly what's going on in the mind of the actor. The actor has two directors: one, the actual director; the other, himself, and that self-director is always with him. So I found that in, say, the first scene with Ariel, while Ariel does a lot of talking (he describes how he created the storm) Prospero stands behind him listening. Now, my usual way was to participate in his description, as if I'm saying "Good boy, Ariel, go to it! Yes!—you did this, and you did that. Fine! That's just what I wanted." Well, that's not wrong, of course as a matter of fact it's suggested by the script. But I found just recently that by composing myself in the way that I've described, by way of the eye and into the Self, that it induced in me a deeper sense of Self as I listened to Ariel. I found it wasn't necessary for me to participate any more. I could just listen and still be much more deeply involved in the nature and quality of my role, a kind of assurance and command which is the very stuff of Prospero.

Yes, but aren't some parts easier to do that in than others? Prospero is often an observer, a prime mover, who then stands back and watches. Lear is so involved in the action, that it must be much more difficult to do what you suggest.

Yes, that's true enough. And Shylock, too. Shylock is always commenting on the action, and he's also deeply involved in it. This example of Prospero is only one of the indications of a way of using the Self. It also connects by way of the imagination with the idea of Prospero being backed up by Shakespeare himself, for the last time saying, "What fools these mortals be."

What is the difference between a free expression of one's Self and the personal mannerisms that one sees in many actors? You touched on this during the lectures, but could you say some more about it?

It's the job, a lifelong job, of an actor, of any artist, I would think, to get down to what is the simplest and the most honest aspect of himself. This work never stops. We sometimes sell ourselves down the river to other people's notions of what we are, so that we find ourselves doing things that might at first be relished by our families, reinforced by our friends, and eventually applauded by our public. These become actor's mannerisms. They're encouraged deliberately in the actor himself in order to please. Well, this is a great mistake in the long run. It is self-deluding, a kind of miniature prostitution. Unfortunately, it *works* at the box office, in the actor's pocket; it works for the producer, but I don't think that's the kind of acting we're talking about. It may be estimable in certain ways. A clown, for example (but then clowning is a different matter), may deliberately employ his bag of tricks because he knows it catches on; but the clown has a marvelous mask which encourages him to grotesqueries which are valid for the part. The kind of idiosyncrasies that we're talking about are those which usually an actor in the act of betraying himself employs in order to be liked, "well liked."

Talking about the clown and his mask, when you did Schweyk (in Brecht's Schweyk in the Second World War), *who is certainly one of the arch-clowns of literature, there was a great deal of Self in that. How does the idea of the mask you used as that character—the nose, the gesture, the sort of perennially innocent smile—relate to the whole sense of inner Self—the composure, and relaxation—that you had?*

You need the inner Self, almost more than ever, in a part like that. Because behind the apparent innocence, the assumed innocence, of a very wise man like Schweyk, which he brings to each scene of the play, there has to be my own understanding of innocence, mine and not yours or the next person's.

How do you relate the personal idiosyncrasies that you found for Schweyk with sense of Self? Did you arrive at them through intuition, observation, experience? What?

Well, as usual, it's a mélange. I remember, for example, a peculiar kind of salute I developed in the part—

A sort of thumbing your nose at authority.

Yes, that's it, but the Nazis in the play could never have accused me of that since the salute was actually a gesture of deference. I know exactly where that came from in my own private storehouse, although I didn't choose it with any great consciousness. It arrived to me from many years ago. I think it was in reading Thomas Hardy, somewhere, that a peasant was described, whenever he talked to the lord of the manor, as having this habit of pulling at his forelock. It was a kind of homely salute, you know. And there it was; until you prompted me just now to tell you where it came from, I hadn't even thought about it. It just arrived, along with the "Spine" of Schweyk. So you see, it *is* a kind of melange. You cannot make the act of acting too mechanical; then you run the risk of really becoming full of quirks and mannerisms. There must always be a kind of residue of life on which you draw. Much of that is unconscious. You must have faith that it'll stand by you; and there's nothing that induces that faith and that belief better than the release of Self. Again I say you must be aware of that three-phase process I mentioned earlier: recognizing, accepting, and then using the Self. Then, after you have worked on all the necessities of the role (your lines and everything else connected with the part), you have the right to call on that same Self again and inform the whole image which you have created with it.

So it starts the process and it ends it.

Yes, that's right.

During the in-between stage, what happens? Must you refer to it constantly?

We all know, we actors, that during the course of rehearsal we lose things. We say "What was it that I did two days ago that I can no longer, apparently, do?" Well, one must have faith, aided and abetted by the director, that the complete image will fill itself out again, and that those things which are valuable will come back to you.

Did you, personally, in your early career have problems with relaxation, problems of Self?

Oh, sure. Oh, certainly.

When did you begin to develop the concept of Self as applied to your own work?

When I was compelled to by the teaching of Stanislavsky, and that happened in the Group Theatre. There I began to realize, just as we realize here again and again, that the element of relaxation was basically important. But before that I had good instincts, I think; I got along in the theatre, even without training, and this was a proof that somehow or other I was performing correctly. And also I had sympathies which were quick. In O'Neill's *Marco Millions* the whole image of the old Khan observing the triviality of Marco Polo, and at the end realizing that there was no quality in the world that equalled love, as he bent over the body of his granddaughter, Kukachin; that kind of thing liberated me very much. And so I could feel that I was capable of acting truthfully up to a certain point. But tension there almost always was; and I don't think I ever accomplished the ultimate performance of all those early parts. It was only when acting followed the line of what Stanislavsky calls "from the conscious to the unconscious," (but what he doesn't say is "from the unconscious back into the conscious") that I really grasped the actor's process. It was only when that was borne in on me and began to prove itself in my work (and I wasn't the only one; all of us Group Theatre people experienced that realization) that I really began to learn, and in learning I began to investigate. That's why teaching is so good for an actor, incidentally, because it forces him to go on and on investigating.

Was there any particular role that began to awaken the concept of Self in you?

I think so. Jacob in *Awake and Sing*. I played it for a long time. We played it in New York, and then we took it on the road; and for me it provided a sort of classic experience in Self.

I used to like to come down and sit on the stage before the curtain went up. This was a mode of preparing myself; here was the place where I was to act; here was the place where I was to live. And one day as I sat in the semi-darkness there on the stage (it was a matinee, I remember, in Cleveland), almost as if I were talking to myself, I said, "Look, you know this part; you know it thoroughly; you could play it standing on your head, or in your sleep. But today I'm going to have you look at people not as if they were the people in the play, but just as themselves. For example, since much of your action has to do with the struggle between yourself and your daughter, played by Stella Adler, when you relate to her today with your eyes, with your voice, with everything, I want you to relate to her knowing that this is Stella. And apply that to everyone; knowing that that's Phoebe; knowing that that's Sandy; that that's Joe; that that's Julie." Well, I did so; and Stella, who in addition to being a marvelous performer is a fine teacher and a great observer of what goes on on the stage, said to me afterwards, "Morris, there was something interesting about what you did today, what was it? Something different." I asked her was it good, and she answered, "Yes, very good, but I don't know what to call it." I said, "Well, let's not give it a name because I'm going to try it again" (like a good scientist, you know). What I think happened was that as I was looking at Stella and recognizing Stella within the Bessie Berger that she was playing, I myself was recognizing my Self, Morris, within Jacob. So that a very lively interchange of personalities took place, so to speak. But this led to intensified Action. I remember that the Actions in the climactic scene with her on that day were exceptionally strong and sharp. Stella recognized it at that particular performance. And in a way, it forces the other actors to do the same thing. If they find a quality of conflict, of antagonism, in me, something in them responds in kind. Well, that was a tentative movement in the direction of Self, a breakthrough for me. And I found after that, that it continued to work. Sounds somewhat mechanical, doesn't it? But it isn't really. Rather *it's a channeling of power—a summons to the full use of yourself.*

Then years later, I played the Mayor in Arthur Miller's version of *An Enemy of the People*; and I had scenes with Fredric March, a couple of fine, strong scenes, collisions. You know how the brothers in that play confront each other and over what issues. I became aware in the process of rehearsal that Fredric March was a charming man; and that, as a matter of fact, he was one of those persons who doesn't have to work so hard; his personal attractiveness works for him, and whatever he does, with whatever special personal edges or mannerisms, whatever you call them, it works; and I must confess that I was a little envious of those qualities. Of course, I couldn't possibly assume any mannerisms, I wouldn't do that for one thing, and for another, I wouldn't know how. But I said to myself, "There's only one thing I can do, and that is to take what he says and does on the most personal level, Self to Self. Give him his Self and let me be my full Self." I tried it; I did it in rehearsal, utterly, completely; especially in those two main scenes that I had with him; and I think it was responsible for the dynamic way in which those scenes played. It was much commented on. So, out of a somewhat shabby motive of wanting to, in a sense, outdo Fredric March at his own game, I learned a great deal about power on the stage. As I say often, the Self is the secret of your power. Well, here I turned it on full force by "pushing buttons" (in a way that's what it is, and there's nothing wrong with that); but I was present as my Self. Complete Morris, if you like, versus complete Fredric; and that confrontation really threw off sparks. It was through that experience, I think, that I really nailed down my whole belief in the use of the Self.

Imagine then, if you have a whole group of actors playing *Three Sisters*, not trying to outdo each other, but all freeing themselves in the way I described, all present with their complete Selves, all of their power, all of their relaxation, all of their human quality, which includes all kinds of extremes, from lovableness to hatefulness, all of those things, then you have life on the stage and Chekhov is reborn.

What was it that prompted you to attempt what appears to me to be quite a risky and almost dangerous experiment with Awake and Sing?

Well, you see, I was confident of the fact that no matter what happened, I couldn't stray very far from the character. As I said before, everything was in place—the words, the movements, the physical characterization, the make-up, all of that—that couldn't possibly be betrayed, no matter what I did.

But you must have been dissatisfied with something?

I *was* dissatisfied with the absence of what I discovered when I made this very connection of Self to Self. I was dissatisfied with the fact that I felt myself acting individually without reference to the requirements of the collective, and I wanted to re-establish that. Not only that, what I must have been dissatisfied with was the very thing which is fed by the discovery of the use of Self—power. By its use I found that the actor becomes a kind of nugget of power. He becomes strong, individualized; and if you have a group of actors all doing the work of the play, all reacting and interacting with each other, liberating their powerful Selves, then you have one hell of a performance.

Can't you have a weak Self?

Yes! You remind me of one of Joyce's characters who says, "Help, I feel a strong weakness." The very weakness of character, let's say of Sam Feinschreiber in *Awake and Sing*, is its strong point for the actor. The actor uses his strong Self to establish a weak character.

Is everyone endowed with a sense of Self, one that can emanate power?

I believe so.

Is power a major ingredient of talent?

Talent comes from so many things. It is stimulated by that whole vast repository of experience, conscious and unconscious, and influenced by all the life and the culture around us.

Also I think talent has to do with the working of that same "muscle" of the imagination that I was talking about. From the very first moment a play is read, if there is anything in that play that calls up your use of imagination, you respond to it. You begin to see things in terms of that play. You begin to identify with parts of it. An excitement takes place. There's a sort of bubbling sensation that goes on in you—a certain stiffening of the spine (I mean the actual spine) which makes you sit up and take notice—a kind of repetition of the phrase, "Yes, I see, I see." And that phrase, "I see," is very significant, because that is what you are doing; you're seeing; you're not only looking, but you're seeing, and that seeing is almost a physical, muscular act. Not only is it propelled by the imagination, but it draws the imagination with it, so that suddenly the whole occasion is lifted onto another level. It's not just the ordinary sitting back and looking, but you're *involved* in the seeing, and that involvement means that your actions are stimulated, because your desires are stimulated, a sign that you are drawn into the life of the play.

Then you begin to make your choices. You choose, "Ah, I'll wear this; I'll look like this; I'll come in haltingly; I'll look at her first before I speak; I'll do this, and I'll do that." The choices begin to relate to the fundamental needs which you perceive in the play as you study it. And the ability to do all this is talent.

I was in *Rocket to the Moon*, Clifford Odets' play. The girl of the play, Cleo, says something really memorable in this regard. In trying to explain herself to the character I was playing, she says, "Talent, I've got talent! It's a feeling . . . that makes me want to dance in my bones." You know, that's pretty darn good. "It makes me want to dance in my bones." Fundamentally, talent is a sort of irresistible rhythm which is set up inside of us, which requires some kind of outlet, perhaps through dance, as Cleo suggests, or more probably it goes even deeper. It expresses a fullness and a desire for release, a desire to put what you know and feel into some kind of form. That I guess comes nearest to any definition of talent that I could give.

When you describe the creative process, it sounds so easy and inevitable. What about discipline? Doesn't it take a great deal of self-discipline to be an actor?

One of the stimuli to creative work is the pleasure of it, not only the rigors, but the acute pleasure. The actor, although he may work very hard and dig very hard, feels a certain pleasure in bringing his instrument, his body and his mind to the service of the work at hand; and so the discipline is of a special character. It involves repetition in rehearsal, following a certain line laid down by all the necessities of the play including the director, of course, and the actors themselves. But I suppose it's the loose nature of it which differentiates the work from that of the sculptor, the painter, or of the writer who forces himself to sit down with his craft at a certain stated time every day. Not that the actor is absolved from that, especially in his formative period when he is really learning about his craft, he has to experiment, he has to test himself as to whether he understands what he's called upon to do.

There is a story about Moskvin, the noted leading actor of the Moscow Art Theatre. He was rehearsing late one night in the theatre; and after rehearsal he left with a friend. They walked together down the street into the snow, and when they were quite a distance from the theatre Moskvin stopped and said, "Will you excuse me? I must go back to the stage and investigate something for myself." That's typical of the needs of the actor. I've done that sort of thing myself, not only to discover what I was looking for in the part, but also to place my voice properly in the auditorium. I've gone on the stage when there was no one around, because there's something about a deserted theatre which is very conducive to creative work and discovery. So as I say, the kind of experimentation and probing that an actor should do with himself is never finished. The discovery of a certain objectivity I spoke of earlier while playing Prospero is something that I'd really never found before. It came, in a sense, by accident; but as Hamlet says, "And therefore as a stranger, give it welcome." So that the actor is always hospitable to such ideas, even when they come unbidden.

Michael Chekhov used to say, "All right, we've worked, we've rehearsed today. We're still in a formative stage. Now, don't push it any more. Go home and sleep on it." This is where it must be admitted, the work of the unconscious really comes in, if you allow it to. Once an actor commits himself to a part, he's really in a sense enslaved. It is his job day and night, even when he's sleeping; and so it's not surprising to expect that certain ideas which have been consciously proposed during the day will now unconsciously root themselves in his understanding and in his whole emotional equipment.

You mentioned at one time when you were beginning to work on King Lear *that you'd put the script down on a chair, and you'd walk around it rather suspiciously. Was that your fear of beginning to throw yourself into the role; or was it an attempt to stand off at the beginning and see it in perspective? Was that discipline or the lack of it? I know*

I've had the same experience; I've hesitated to start on a project because I felt it was a little overwhelming at the beginning.

Well, of course, any job of work in the theatre is a mighty job. A part as mighty as Lear inspires awe. I think that was my first reason for stalking the part. I would put the book on the chair or a table and just find myself walking around the room like a cat, looking at this thing—"What is it?"—as if it contained a secret or a mystery, which indeed it did. In fact, the whole approach to *Lear* emanated like the smoke out of Aladdin's lamp with a certain mysterious feeling and mysterious atmosphere. The "stalking" represented both awe and expectation as well as a fear of making a preliminary mistake, an initial error.

An irrevocable commitment, in a sense?

Well, you know that you're going to be irrevocably committed to it once you've been given the part; that's that. But it's like engaging a woman in a love affair. Unless you're a very secure or even brutal lover, you make your approaches tentatively, because you are really trying to find out about her, giving her a chance to find out about you. You don't want to involve yourself mistakenly with a part. Also don't forget, you are committing yourself to the actor's act of finding your Spine. You know that it's somewhere within the clay, the marble; and as yet you don't know what it is. You're not able to give it a local habitation and a name, but you know it is there; and the more practiced you are as an actor, you also know that before not too long you will come up with what is central about the part. So often in Shakespeare, the beginning of everything is a sense of mystery, which I believe that Shakespeare himself shared with us. I mean he himself had it. There's something foggy and misty that hangs over plays like *A Midsummer Night's Dream* and *As You Like It*, even *The Tempest*. Although there the process of human plotting and rascality by which Prospero came to the island is revealed to you, it's the misty things of life and of experience that bring him in the end to true wisdom.

A play is a curious thing. Almost of its own volition, it would seem, it reveals its secrets as you go on probing. The play is full of juices; it's full of stimulation and full of secrets; and it will yield them up to you if you continue to probe. Sooner or later, as in the case of Shylock for example, one determining factor will happen or suggest itself around which everything suddenly falls into place.

Isn't it sometimes the sense of commitment, a sense of "feeling one's oats," that allows the Self to emerge freely and easily; whereas, for example, the awful insecurity of an unemployed actor attempting an audition tends to shrivel up that sense of Self?

That's certainly true, but the Self need not allow itself to be shriveled. I'm not saying, Peter, that the Self is always rambunctious and arrogant, by any means;

the Self is the fullest person that you're capable of being. This involves not only visions of glory and great fulfillment, but also tenderness: the merest kind of response to Objects, their beauty, their possibilities, their tragedy, a whole spectrum of feelings that are available to you once you have confidence in yourself. I admit that the people I mentioned in the office looking for work were moving in an atmosphere in which those very qualities tend to be shriveled up. When you are thinking about bread and butter and soup, you're not in a very "artistic" frame of mind. But I don't think that what I suggest should be dismissed as simply a consummation devoutly to be wished. It may take quite a long time to develop this sense of Self. It comes as the fruit of your tree, not as the first tentative sprouting of the leaves; in other words, I believe, after you have really grasped your job as an actor, and you know what you can do. Later when you add the ingredient of your full, untrammelled individuality, then is when the juices, the sap, begin to flow into the tree.

You make me harken back to the memory of the very first play I was ever in. I played the title role in *Disraeli* in high school; and apparently I was good for my age. Young as I was, I must have given a good account of myself. (I'd give anything to see that performance today.) But from that event on, I became someone, a "person." Before that I was in "standing water," as Shakespeare says. I was not very secure in myself, but then suddenly I became aware that I was special—that I could perform: walk on a stage, say lines (however I said them), and win a certain amount of attention. Fortunately, I didn't become conceited; but perhaps it foreshadowed the possibility of a sense of Self. As you see, I surround everything with "perhaps" and "maybe," because up to the time that I made the final craft discoveries in the Group Theatre, I wasn't sure of anything as a far as a basis of craft was concerned. Now at least I'm reasonably sure.

In those days I was very aware of myself and even encouraged in myself certain (what shall I call them) vibrations. I knew I could respond emotionally to many things. When I was alone, certain things would go through my mind; I found I would cry easily; I was sensitive. I would say, incidentally, that that kind of releasing mechanism in one is also a sign of talent in answer to your earlier question. It's like a machine, a car that idles without really being directed, before it's in gear: you're ready to go, the car is trembling and full of the possibility of movement.

In the subsequent years at college and so on, when I would be cast in plays, there was a kind of exhibitionistic fervor about some of the things that I did. I'm sure that I must have been very funny in certain ways, but I was bold. I didn't scruple about overdoing, which indicates that I must have had some kind of interior image of the part I was playing. For example, in a terrible play called *If I Were King*, I played Louis XI; and for the first time I used some sort of contortion of my shoulders, limping about the stage. I don't know if that's historically accurate, but I found myself using my hands in a wild and wooly way and rather enjoying it. No one stopped me, which perhaps was fortunate because my boldness was being served, and I had the nerve to attempt these things. Even then I wasn't sure that I would go on the stage, but something in me, way down, said, "Yes, you are; if it can be done, you're going on the stage." When I came to the end of my college career, certain friends of mine said "Go, and don't look back. None of your Lot's-wife-business, you *go*! Go right away." I allowed myself to be persuaded.

How did you manage during your early career to maintain some kind of perspective on yourself and your work?

Well, I'm glad that in the early part of my acting life, I didn't feel under the obligation of making a pile of money. I just didn't care about it. I had a certain idealism, which was a random idealism, idealism in general; and it did not include the necessity to make a fortune, and so I would take chances. For example, I had six fairly happy, financially solid years with the Theatre Guild, but through it all there was a nagging sense that I wasn't altogether the craftsman that I wanted to be. There was no opportunity of *learning* until the Group Theatre idea came along; I, without hesitation, threw my lot in with that, even though I was doing very well at the Guild.

You never studied acting before that?

No, not really, I worked for a short while with a fine character actor, Emmanuel Reicher, whose reputation was based on Ibsen and Sudermann; and he used to put us through our paces in scenes from those two playwrights, mainly; but in spite of that, I felt that there was no foundation all along the line. And then, of course, at that time we began to hear from Europe about all kinds of new things that were taking place there, primarily about the Stanislavsky system and the Moscow Art Theatre; we yearned to see those actors, and even without seeing them, to be like them. Therefore, we were pretty agitated with the hope of extending ourselves when it came to the idea of forming a Group Theatre. So, this ability to plunge into something, even though I didn't know how it would turn out, was something that luckily worked out for about ten years in the Group Theatre.

A fortunate naivete, in a way.

Yes, we all "suffered" from it, except for our directors. They sensed what we were in for; they were a little wiser in the ways of Broadway than we were, more objective.

It seems to me that your sense of Self flourished in the conducive atmosphere of the Group Theatre because there was a feeling of love, of commitment to a purpose over

and above yourself; discovering a system of acting and expressing a social con-
sciousness.

That's true.

And on the other hand, if I may bring it up, during the dark period of blacklisting,
when it was very difficult for you to find work, was your sense of Self very much in-
jured?

No, on the contrary, Peter. This is the interesting thing about that period. Just
as in a much more trivial way I discovered that I was a person after doing my
first play in high school, so the exacerbating influence, the effect of that
blacklisting business, was in a curious way a strengthener. It showed people
what they were. It showed them in a negative way, too, what they could *not*
do—what they *would* not do. The true meaning of freedom, free will, free conscience, was borne in on many of the people, and in my small way, and I say it
again, it was a small way, I felt it too. It amounted to this: I was able to say,
"No! You can push me so far, but beyond that I simply cannot go." No heroism
is involved here. It was a simple human discovery I made about myself; and in
the confrontation, the unpleasantness of the confrontation before the Com-
mittee, there was a kind of process which is very much the actor's process—a
summary of "what have we here? Who are my Objects? Who are the people
who are judging me? What are they like?"—and I remember distinctly their
cynical, sophisticated, sometimes stupid—childish even—faces, as they sat there
ready to be not only my judge, but everybody else's. There happened on that
day a piece of testimony from a chap who was, from my point of view,
disgusting. He was willing to spill names, willing to divulge all; and I could see,
in looking around the room, the reaction of disgust, not only on the faces of
people that I knew, but also people whom I had never seen before—reporters
for papers—they listened to this man who was spilling his guts; and you could
see revulsion in their faces. I wasn't making it up; there it was. And so at any
rate, one of the things that one has to fight for is one's sense of self respect.

But what about afterwards when you couldn't find work?

As I say, my sense of Self was more assured than ever. I say it without vanity;
there's no sense in being vain about a thing like that. That was a damned
unpleasant experience somewhat like the way you take a stone and rub it on
sandpaper to bring out its sheen. Something of the sort happened. And I
wasn't the only one. We learned who our friends were, and in a word, we knew
where we stood. We knew who our enemies were—our deep-down enemies—we
knew what was admirable; we knew what was disgusting. In a way, it was a
Shakespearean experience. You see, it took in all the extremes of human

character; it was epic. So there you were, left with this precious residue of realization in you which came unbidden out of an ugly experience.

Did you find that in other adverse situations, when things weren't going well for you, that your sense of Self was threatened?

It may have had a few jolts, Peter, but I don't think very serious things were threatened. I was always lucky in that I've always had a self-encouraged love of music, books, and matters like that in general, and friends; and so the basic life of which I was capable, although not always encouraged by accomplishment in art or in craft, continued to be pretty much what I always had planned for.

Of course it may happen that certain individuals, whether they know about Self or not, allow themselves to be ground out, ground down, by events. This, of course, leads to a larger area of surmise and speculation. Suppose we had a theatre which encouraged this thing that we call sense of Self, what a rich theatre that would be! And suppose we had a society surrounding that same theatre, which also allowed the Self to be simple and free. Well, the imagination absolutely boggles trying to envisage the possibilities.

Doesn't it take social ferment to produce the kind of immediate commitment and vitality that such a theatre reflects, as we said about the Group Theatre? I'm sure that the Elizabethan age was a tremendously vital age with all sorts of conflict and aggression—the kind of ferment that produced the theatre in which a Shakespeare could develop.

Nevertheless, I don't think that it was conscious in the way that the Group Theatre was when it started. The Group Theatre knew what it was in for; and it did so by recognizing the world that it was born into. I remember very distinctly that Harold Clurman went to great pains to describe the responsibilities of a theatre like the one we were contemplating: how every element of the theatre had to be understood as contributing to the final Spine, you might say, the Action, of the theatre.

Which was?

Well, at the outset, our theatre stated that we were committing ourselves to American plays with a social purpose, preferably those that would mirror and suggest the possible amelioration of our life as a people. That for us was a sufficient commitment. We understood that; we went ahead to serve it. One of the first means, of course, was to transform ourselves as craftsmen, as artists; and in doing so, we found that we had to transform ourselves as people very often, because the air was full of all kinds of social pressures and speculations, and you couldn't escape consideration of those things. I myself was on cloud nine when

I joined the Group Theatre. I was aware that the world around us was changing drastically, and of course we were in the middle of a depression—the Depression. But it was only by the kind of plays that we were doing at that time, and the kind of talk that was going on all around us, that I began to realize that I was part of a very critically changing world, and that willy-nilly I couldn't escape it—there it was, I may as well face up to it. Now I doubt whether this kind of thinking went on in Shakespeare's time at the Globe, but I do think that Shakespeare was a great revolutionary. I don't think it was conscious in him, but look at the contrast, look at the sheer, amazing, miraculous contrast between his plays and the plays which preceded him. Compare *Hamlet* with *Everyman*.

I agree with you, there was a terrific ferment going on in his day, an expression of individualism and freedom. I think the Renaissance ideal of the free man was almost arrogantly in the air when Shakespeare wrote; and he expressed character in his plays with that arrogant freedom prevailing around him. That's why I think he was revolutionary. And in light of Shakespeare's accomplishments I ask myself these days, are we producing the kind of theatre that is really breaking new ground, really ploughing down deep, or are we just scratching away on the surface of things? I think the world of the theatre is waiting for some powerful and reverberating voice to speak, but I don't know where it's going to come from.

Do you think in this day and age that it's natural for people to come together in an audience and watch a theatrical presentation, especially when they can sit alone in front of their TV's?

It always has been. People come together and watch anything, even a street accident. The unique thing about the theatre is the presence of the human body. There it is, up on the stage, and here we other bodies are, down here. There's a peculiar kind of vibration that takes place between the listeners and the doers, which makes it a very human experience, fragile and easily destroyed. But there is a special pleasure in an audience coming to see a company that they know, performing a new play or performing an old one well, simply because they know those actors, because they have come to share a human experience with them. If they've seen me before as Lear or Shylock, they recognize me. They know it is I who am up there on the stage, and I'm very willing to share my "I-ness" with them. And that's part of the pleasure—and the necessity, for I continue to claim that the only avenue to conveying what the play is about is by means of the human being as actor expressing his humanity in technical terms, and by technique you already know I mean life terms. I don't see any other way. When a person writes a play (Shakespeare is a prime example), he writes human beings for human beings. So, while there are many ways of displaying this jewel and examining its facets from all directions, fundamentally the nugget in the center is human experience and human feelings.

. . . which is all finally that the actor and the audience can relate to together.

Exactly. The silence that I sometimes heard when I would walk down the stairs after being defeated in the courtroom in *The Merchant of Venice*, the thick, heartbroken kind of silence, was the greatest criticism I ever received in my life.

In Chekhov's *Swan Song*.
L. to r.: Will Lee and Morris Carnovsky.

The Actors' Lab production of *Awake and Sing*, 1946.
L. to r.: Morris Carnovsky and John Garfield.

An Enemy of the People, directed by Robert Lewis, 1950.
L. to r.: Morris Carnovsky, Fredric March, Florence Eldridge,
Fred Stewart, Martin Brooks.

The Brandeis University production of
Schweyk in the Second World War,
directed by Peter Sander, 1967.

As Firs in the Long Wharf Theatre
production of *The Cherry
Orchard*, 1983.

Actor's Choices:
The Search for Spine

How is it that you never did any Shakespeare before 1956 when you appeared in King John?

Well, there was always the promise in the Group Theatre, that we would eventually do the classics; but the nearest we got to it was an attempt to do *Three Sisters* in our very last summer. And that fell through. As a matter of fact, the Group Theatre ended on that note. But, there is no question that the impulse the Group Theatre gave all our work, and certainly my own, was what guided us in the direction of the possibility of doing the classics. Of course, I always wanted to do Shakespeare; so that when I actually came to the doing of it, the ground for *technical preparation* was there. The twig was bent and I couldn't think along other lines except those which we had established in the Group.

While I was with the Theatre Guild, there was an abortive attempt to do *Much Ado About Nothing*. It was directed by Robert Edmond Jones, who prepared a very beautiful production, but it never came to anything. That's the closest I ever came to it. So, when John Houseman called me up and asked me to do a part in *King John*, it was like plunging a magnet into a bunch of iron filings: the ideas surrounding the impulse to do Shakespeare began to coagulate, and I immediately began to think in terms which I was accustomed to, namely, action, atmosphere, all the technical elements we had inherited from the Group experience.

It was only after beginning to tackle the part that I began to see that you couldn't tangle with the part unless you tangled with the play. That is, even if Salisbury, which I played, was a character in his own right, he was inescapably a part, a color, a facet of the entire play. The play, after all, is called *King John*; and it contains enormous activity and some very unusual characters such as the Bastard Faulconbridge, who is the real "king" in the play. Well, Salisbury was a small role comparatively, but all the more reason why I found it necessary to ask myself, how does he fit into the large design?

I remember when I came to the first rehearsal of the play, I was intensely curious about what was going to take place. Houseman was directing, and there were some darn good people in the cast. They were mature actors, all of great experience. I sat in the outer room listening to the scene that was being done, and something in me began to instinctively disagree, even rebel. I heard the age-old accents, you know, of the old fashioned actor: the induced thunder, so to speak, of the voice, and it struck me as so unreal and exhibitionistic. Here again was the old tendency of the actors' throwing themselves into it, "having a bash at it" as the English actors put it, and saying, "what the hell, the music of the piece, the drumrolls, the clash of arms, and the great confrontations, those will see you through. Shakespeare has seen to that. All you have to do is learn your lines and deliver them with the right *ping* and there it is." I said to myself, perhaps not consciously, but it certainly occurred to me, "I can't do that. I cannot do that kind of acting," if it is to be called acting. Those actors were not *talking* to each other, and you know what an emphasis I lay on talking. I said to myself, "They're not connecting. It's each man for himself, but not each man *with* himself connected with the other Self." And so while I wasn't terribly clear about how I was to behave, myself, in that situation, I am sure that something in me began to grope toward some sort of solution. And it was only after playing the part and thinking at it constantly, and impelled, I think, by a kind of "monistic" thing in me which perhaps comes from my early Orthodox Jewish training, that I began to look for a *central idea* in the play. This search for a central idea is, I think, the thing that has dominated all my subsequent work.

As a result of my own particular investigations, what I came up with was the very last statement in the play by the Bastard. It goes, "Nought shall make us rue,/ If England to itself do rest but true." What seemed involved in that as far as my own character, Salisbury, was concerned, was something that I think applied to all of the characters, the English characters in the play; and that is 'fidelity'—the idea of being true to yourself and to England. "To thine own self be true"—perhaps *King John* is the earliest statement of that in Shakespeare; this is what the Bastard stands for, and this is eventually what brings Salisbury, in spite of the defection of which he *is* guilty, back into the fold. "For he is an Englishman," you know, without *Pinafore's* comic overtones. This must have reverberated in Shakespeare's consciousness. And while I'm not sure he started out to make a play around that theme, he found himself drawn into it as he wrote, so that as an Englishman, he was traversing the path that only a good Englishman could.

In rehearsal at first I may not have assigned significance to those last two lines but later it was like a seal on everything that I had found to do which emanated from the truth of the action. Nothing will succeed unless it's true.

Did you find that this whole question of Spine was reinforced by working in

Shakespeare for the first time, or was it a revelation for you that it also applied to the acting of Shakespeare's plays?

It's always a revelation. It was a vitally interesting revelation because I began to form out of the new experience of playing in Shakespeare the fundamental simplicity of my whole approach to *any* part. The roots were there. I had experienced them, had made all the fundamental discoveries when I was working in the Group. I had learned how to make contact with people and things, the use of the Object. I had learned how to relax, even if only physically, superficially; how to really look at Objects; and how to listen to people. All the elements of the Stanislavsky method as it was revealed to us at the time. I was at any rate conscious of them, but the more I worked in Shakespeare, the more intense was the attention to these things, and later I found, by working on such roles as Shylock and Prospero (not yet Lear), that the whole mass of Stanislavskian teaching could be summed up and contained in a very simple formula.

Why do you think that American actors who do have, to some extent, a developed sense of truth, have such difficulty with Shakespeare?

Well, I think American actors, coming as they do from so many different regional influences, are a little afraid of speech, particularly poetic speech. There's a tendency I think among American actors to suspect any "fancy" approach to words. Now as it happens in my own case, I love words, I always did; for me a word is a very living and exciting thing. Much of the pleasure of reading Shakespeare, let alone acting him, is to realize the sheer magic of these words being put together. Almost anywhere you put your finger, even in the earlier plays of Shakespeare, there's excitement: something dynamic about the words inflates us, excites and uplifts us. This is the sensation I learned to look for in myself, a kind of movement inside me which said, "My God, who talks like that? Well, I'm going to talk like that because Shakespeare told me to!" Whenever that happens there's a kind of lifting of the entire consciousness. You can't reduce that kind of impulse, you can't subdue it and subjugate it to a customary American way of speech. Somehow or other you've got to find a kind of "plangency" to language which makes it resound, which makes it really become the container of the tremendous Actions that exist in Shakespeare.

Do you think some people are just born "word-aware"—or can that quality be developed?

I think it can be learned. As Prospero says to Caliban, "I endowed thy *purposes* with words that made them known." I don't think it ought to be a special gift, this response to words. I personally, for example, began to notice the differences in style between foreign languages, French and English, German and

English, Italian and English, and Latin and English. I was intrigued by the character, the sheer character, of the various languages. I remember there was a small story I read in an Italian course in college, and it had a title which I latched onto as the most beautiful words I had ever heard in my whole life. The name of the piece was *The Sardinian Drummer Boy*; in Italian it was *Il Tamburino Sardo*. I used to go along the streets of St. Louis, adapting those words to a phrase out of *Scheherezade*. I would sing them, when I was alone, and I used to love the sound and sensation of it. So music is involved too, the ear for music. The very sound of French, you know, "Allons enfants de la Patrie, le jour de gloire," and so on. A dramatic, elevating kind of sound. And then: "Nel mezzo del cammin di nostra vita/mi ritrovai per una selva oscura." Those Italian sounds linger in the mind; I use them constantly to stimulate myself. I do it now before going on as Prospero. I stand off stage and murmur those marvelous words from Dante's *Inferno* to myself.

What was the first role in which you began to realize that the character was subservient to a larger concept, one that ran underneath the lines and shaped everything in the play?

I think it goes pretty far back. I remember doing the part of the Old Khan in O'Neill's *Marco Millions*. There was an opportunity, through humanity and love, for an experience which I treasured in myself. That part liberated me and gave me assurance for other such parts in the future. All I know is that the desire to become emotionally free has always been with me. I think I wanted to "make" emotion. I wanted to be like some of the early Yiddish actors that I used to see on the stage. Unbridled emotion. I was thrilled by the fact that they could free themselves to that extent: they could cry as they wanted to and be utterly and completely and vibratingly alive. I wanted to be like that; and at the beginning I made the usual mistake, I am sure, of a young actor, attempting to "turn it on," which in some ways was better than nothing, but it was wrong; as I began to discover when the original emotion which I strained to produce rebelled, and tension took its place. It was the whole encounter with Stanislavsky's teaching much later that gave me the tool with which to cope with the summoning of emotion. You and I know that you just cannot turn it on. That emotion must be wooed, charmed, invited. Some people can "turn it on," but that's a sometime thing. It'll come sometimes and other times it won't. A well-chosen, meaningful Spine will help in harnessing and liberating the emotions. For example, Falstaff's Spine, as I saw it, in the production of *Henry IV, Part One* which we did together, is "the love of life." His comments on honor make it very clear what he thinks about that concept by contrast with the notion of love and life. Who wants to die? he says. Who wants to fight? To kill? When there's sack and women and good fellowship. What are we here for? There you have an inflaming idea. That, as Falstaff, sends the blood to my cheeks. I can almost feel it. A properly chosen Spine should be able to stimulate many impulses to *Action*. The mark of a good Spine, I think, is that it does that. The actor playing Salisbury in *King John*, for example, is called upon to weep at the death of young Arthur. The Spine of "No, I'm an Englishman, that is my whole duty, and I will remain that until I die" is a self-inflaming idea that leads to that emotional response.

Moreover the Spine provides a key to the character's underlying Action or inner conflict. Salisbury is *struggling to find* a unity in himself. Until he does find it, he's an unresolved character. He's at war with himself. And that's the pretext of *King John*: England at war with itself.

The actor's Spine, so to speak, holds the play erect.

That's right; that's good. By the way, it occurred to me while we were talking just now, that usually the place to look for the naked Spine—and a Spine should be naked—is the high point of the play or the high point of the character. This, of course, is arguable. I have found that the true high point is not always readily found, but in digging for the Spine, I think you have to come to the point where you say, "This, this is the center of radiation; this is the height of my action, here in the play."

Even if you're a minor character?

Yes. Oh, yes. Every character. Which sounds as if it's all supposed to be very emotional, but that depends on the character and the circumstances, of course. It's up to the actor to find what his high point is. Whatever will feed him. Yes, it's like a fountain, which feeds, to mix a metaphor. So that when I found that center for Shylock that we discussed in the lectures there were no more problems. I knew where I was, what I was; I knew what I would do, what I had done; I knew the world I lived in.

Spine simply defined is the reason for all your actions. Since actions are not exerted by keeping them within, they seek an Object. Example: "I hate you." You're my Object. "I intend to eradicate you." You're still my Object. My intention is really from me to you, to annihilate you. Now I find myself boiling a little bit with the reasons why. "You spit upon my Jewish gabardine" again. The Spine is the reason for everything because it provides you with the most impulses to action.

How does the character's Spine fit into the central theme of the play? What, for instance, is the Spine of the Merchant of Venice?

I would call its theme the corruption that breeds from money, and my particular choice of Shylock's Spine, namely, his response to having been spat on, worked for me constantly within the circumstances born out of money and the corruption that stems therefrom. "You, Antonio, are tarred with the same brush that I am. Money. I'm tarred with the same brush as Portia. Money. We are all marked by it, but it's sublimely easy for you, Antonio, to spit on me. Does this make you a better person? By the fact that I am profoundly affronted and respond with indignation, *I* think that makes *me* a better person than you are. I'm a man."

How much of a play's theme and your Spine come to you intuitively and how much by analysis?

The "formula," which is the basic substance of our discussions, is intended as an aid to thought. Of course, I must emphasize that no formula will absolve the actor from the lifelong performance of tasks that continue to test his sense of truth and the responsibility to himself as an instrument.

But you ask about intuition. Of course what a play exposes and what an actor grasps is really the visible part of the iceberg. The rest is below, and that's in some ways the more important part, the unconscious; and in acting Shakespeare, the great, almost glorious venture is to attempt to merge your unconscious as an actor with Shakespeare's vast unconscious. There's where "actor's scholarship" belongs.

And how do you do that?

Through unforced feeling, through sympathy—there's the word sympathy,—"withfeeling," feeling with. That's how. And that's why, incidentally, it is especially necessary for the actor to be developed as a human being.

I think that an actor should be aware of how sensitive he is as a person, and therefore as an instrument. He should believe in his own belief, so to speak; that is to say, he should learn to love what he is doing; he should learn to love what the other person is doing, even though these two people are as opposite as Iago and Othello; and this will enable him to perceive *Objects*, which are prime, I think, in the consideration of this business of stimulating yourself. I've spoken about that moment in *Hamlet* when Hamlet says, "My father. Methinks I see my father." Well, if he's concentrated enough, if he's achieved "public solitude," we call it, sufficiently, if he is aware that the trans-action which takes place is now between himself and the memory of his beloved father, to the degree that he is aware of that, it will excite him. So that moment, and you know I emphasize that any job of acting is a succession of moments, that moment then merges humanly and naturally into the next moment. It's almost as if the love for the father (I feel it as I speak) is transferred in the subsequent moment to the love of Horatio, his only friend; and that makes a bridge of Action, which then carries on to the next thing—the revelation,—"Saw?

Who?". . ."The king, my father,". . ."Tell me, tell me."—and gives me, even as I do it now, a different feeling of that moment than I've ever had before. For me the whole impulse into the scene with Horatio comes still from that previous moment, "My father. Methinks I see my father." It all stems from a willingness to surrender to suggestion from the Object.

Michael Chekhov once said, Since we, as actors, are instruments, there should be no difficulty about crying or laughing, if those are the two extremes by which we judge ourselves. For example . . . and he began to cry! He "turned it on" like mad. Tears. "Distraction in's aspect, a broken voice" and so on, the whole business. And almost immediately switching from that, he said, "And is it more difficult to laugh?" And he began to laugh so hysterically that the whole classroom was turned into a house of laughter. And that was simply, I think, because he had instant reflexes and responses to Objects. He might think about anything, a dead bird or something like that, and it excited all of his molecules so to speak. It's physical, complete. Sometimes, Peter, the teaching of acting, the gospel of acting according to St. Stanislavsky, is made a little mechanical. "Thus shall you do, and the result shall be this. You put it in here, and it comes out there." That's wrong. I think the freedom of the actor should be encouraged, a feeling of pleasure, and of love for what he does. Almost the first exercise in any play should be, "Look at each other. Just look. Appreciate each other, and never let that appreciation down."

And all that begins with the element of Will. It's the Will on the stage that makes it possible for you to *willingly* respond to your own feeling of ease or relaxation or sense of Self, to your own appreciation of Objects, to your own understanding, say, of how you should walk as the character, to your understanding of how you are wearing your costume, to the whole business of the conscious appreciation of yourself in all of its aspects. That's the readiness and so much more. And then all I have to do is say, "*I am me.*" "I am now ready; I'll go on; I'll walk on that stage." Remember the "significant" walking exercise that we did in class. "I will find an Object—I *connect*, as I as Prospero do with that toy ship next to me on stage at the beginning of *The Tempest*. Now I will shift my eyes to my magic cloak. I am now putting it on, and the music which plays at this point I allow to help me. I am magical now, with the cloak on. I turn back to the little ship; I pick it up"; and the play is on because I am now in the process of shattering Alonso's fleet. Prospero's "darker purpose" has begun.

In a way you allow your naïveté and your childlike belief to take over.

Definitely.

But that's often very difficult for a young actor. Many of them resist with something like, "Oh, come on. A magic cloak."

Well, but that's inartistic. The magic cloak is given to you as one of the circumstances of the play. To reject it is inartistic. If you believe there's no sense to what a character does, to what you do, to what you're being asked to do, then perhaps you're not the actor for the part. But I think that's a minor matter. Usually if a play has been chosen for its quality, that quality takes for granted a certain logic, verisimilitude; and people are people, they're not mannequins that move for no reason or because the director tells them to. Furthermore if actors demand that they not be just puppets or pawns that are picked up and shoved around, then they've got to participate in the artistic creative life of rehearsal by finding out what the play is really about so they can serve that purpose. You see I was brought up, in a sense, by Harold Clurman who is my idea of a fine director. What I particularly love about him is that his exposure of the possibilities of the play from the very beginning is so clear, so unusual. He exposes the play in a way that you may never have thought of; and this is exciting. What then happens in the process of rehearsal has to justify those first two days of precious wonderful talk. As far as I'm concerned, it always stimulates me; and after that I know that I have to find my own way in order to serve the same illumination that he's given me.

Do you usually find your own way, that is, the Spine of the part right away?

Not usually, but when you do find it, and you find it properly, then that is it, and everything you do after that is related to it. A most interesting example occurs to me out of my own work. I was playing the dentist Ben Stark in *Rocket to the Moon* by Odets. I really don't think I was cast properly in that play, as I see it, after all these years. However there I was, playing it, and I knew in the course of rehearsals that somehow or other I wasn't filling the bill. And try as I might, I couldn't find what the trouble was; and the directors couldn't either. I say "directors" because Harold Clurman was there and Clifford himself. We were aware of the fact that they talked things over between themselves. And by the nature of the criticism I received from them, I was feelingly aware that I wasn't somehow right,—I wasn't good; I hadn't found it. Well, the fact was, I hadn't. I hadn't found anything that would serve *me* as a Spine. It was easy enough to say that my Spine was "to find love," which in a way it was; but that in itself wasn't doing it for me. It didn't mean anything to me. Of course it does mean a lot to me, it means a lot to everyone, but in the circumstances of that particular play, it didn't. I was pretty desolate as you may imagine. Well, it was our habit, a very good habit as you know, on the day of the opening to sit in a very relaxed way and just simply talk the play to each other. It was a kind of last reminder of all our work: what we had done here; what we had done there; what the lines were, and so on. I was doing this and listening to the play; and suddenly I heard Luther Adler as my father-in-law in the play—he was talking to someone else *about* the character I was playing—he said something like,

"Well, you know, when he was a boy he didn't have any parents and they put him in some sort of children's home, and he was there until he grew up, around 14 or 15." And I suddenly heard this, having heard it every day in rehearsal; but I heard it *fresh*, for the first time; and I realized in a flash, because that's how these thoughts work, that this was basically important. I didn't have time to prove it by rehearsal. We were about to open that night. But I said, for better or worse, that's what I am going to take for my Spine. That comment about being in an orphan asylum provided me with a powerful image. I saw myself as a boy, an innocent, yearning boy, which I still am in the play even though I am a married dentist. I saw myself as that same boy looking out at the world through bars. The image of this, combined with everything I already knew about Ben Stark, was very moving; and it accounted for my relationship to my father-in-law, whom I regard as a scamp and a cynic but whom I like very much; my relationship to the girl in the office; especially my relationship to my wife, a difficult marriage, tainted somehow or other by the image of those bars, the yearning toward life, at the same time being separated from it, and so with my relationship to everything in the play. That's why I say the Spine is that which will excite in the actor the greatest number of Actions. Well, all I can tell you is that I played it that way that night deliberately. It was the most deliberate and conscious act of technical playing that I had ever done. I played it that way right to the end, and it worked, even superficially it worked in the fact that the reviews for me were splendid, highly unexpected.

I'm interested in your use of the word "technical." That always means to me voice and speech, movement, and perhaps the kind of organization of a role without internal intuitive involvement; and yet you say you performed technically.

By technical, I mean observance of all the means that we actors use. As you know, with me the word technical is a very juicy word. It's a creative word, and it doesn't mean mechanical.

The voice, the movement, and all that, I take for granted. That has its own technique, the technique of voice production and so on. It's absolutely essential, but my use of the word has much more to do with inner behavior coupled with outer activity in the midst of a group of given circumstances.

Would you call that craft or intuition?

Craft provides the means whereby intuition may be released. I never put it that way before, but I think it's true. In a sense we're always pushing buttons in ourselves. "The readiness is all," Hamlet says; and that readiness waits upon the work of the actor; when you push the "right button," the readiness comes forth and happens. If I ever feel stale or non-attentive to the beauty of my daughter in our current *Tempest*, I refresh myself by looking at her. She has lovely eyes and very interesting other elements so there's a lot to look at. But having looked, I don't stay with it, I have re-established connection: it's the work of a second. That's a very superficial example of one of the many ways by which we can recall ourselves to full duty, which is to free the *readiness* in us.

That takes a lot of experience.

It does, but I've never been able to admit that young actors or actresses can't respond to these ideas fully, immediately, if they're sensitive enough. They do, as a matter of fact, in their way. For example this same girl in *Tempest* is capable of doing a variety of things; and I'll bet she doesn't give technique or craft as I talk about it, a tuppence worth of attention. She knows that when she comes on and looks in a certain way and composes her body in a certain way, she's as attractive as the play fundamentally needs. I'm not running down her talent either but she has more in her than meets the eye. There's more to her, and it has never been tapped.

How do you tap that?

By study, by urging. By holding her to a serious course of training.

Apropos Prospero, you know I talk about trying to find the Spine wherever I can, whether it be an active verb or a descriptive suggestion from the author as in the case of Shylock or a descriptive suggestion given by another character. It's a curious thing; the other day I read the chapter on *The Tempest*, called *Prospero's Staff*, in Jan Kott's book, *Shakespeare Our Contemporary.** In a kind of mixture of surprise and elation I found echoed there a very important detail I have been working with during my perfromance in the role. Kott draws a relationship between the whole character of Prospero as delineated by Shakespere—his attitude toward magic; to the problems of the play; to his whole world, the medieval Renaissance world—and a certain self-portrait of Leonardo da Vinci. I had had that thought myself, independently; and suddenly I found it confirmed by what he said. In my dressing room I keep a book called *500 Self-Portraits*; there that da Vinci portrait is. So that among the things which I may do before I go on as Prospero, I will say "Nel mezzo del cammin di nostra vita, etc. . . ," there's something freeing about that; and I will recall the face of da Vinci. Now of course if I only imitate the portrait because of certain lines about the eyes and mouth and all that, that's nonsense. Superficial. But I try to grasp something that is the secret of that bitterness and anguish in the portrait, and I find that something does come to me which is very moving and

*Kott, Jan. *Shakespeare, Our Contemporary.* Garden City, N.Y.: Anchor Books, Doubleday and Co., Inc., 1966.

strengthening at the same time. Kott quotes a written question of Leonardo's: "Leonardo, to what end do you labor?" And there is this in his eyes and the lines about his mouth. A severe judging of the values of life. You see it; it's all there, every bit of it. And I have taken that practically as my Spine in the doing of this play. I believe that this is the reason that many of the reviewers have said about me, "He's too patriarchal; he's too severe. There must be some fun in doing magic. Why doesn't he show us what fun it is rather than doing it so seriously." Well, in the light of my understanding of what that portrait of da Vinci gives me, no, there's no fun in magic; there's no fun in the discovery of evil; there's no fun in surveying human character; there's no fun in living a life which irrevocably ends in a useless death. Where then is the solution? The solution can only be in a *return to life* as Prospero does at the end of the play and like a pack horse assumes the burdens of an encroaching old age. Having established his beloved daughter in her proper place, he returns to Milan where "Every third thought, " he says, "shall be my grave." That's what I find in that face of da Vinci, and much more that I just can't do. All this is another example of how the Spine is found.

Which even now, I see, affects you.

Yes, yes. What I've just done is perhaps an example of how to work with your students. Take a portrait, a piece of music, or a poem and really examine it; then try to merge with it, because you don't choose an action or Spine mechanically, or intellectually even. It's an emotional choosing really. In the case of Shylock certainly. In the case of the dentist in *Rocket to the Moon.*

It's a discovery which comes from your work on the play. In rehearsal you have worked day after day on the truths, on the little truths of the play: how to run a dentist's office; whom to welcome into it and whom to bar from it. How one relates to a dangerous intrusion by a certain person, let's say the girl who eventually threatens Ben Stark's marriage by causing him, in a way, to fall in love with her. All these things are the simpler activities of a play, but the fundamental motor that makes everything chug and move to its conclusion, this is the impelling motive, the *emotional* impelling motive. This is won through the suffering of rehearsal.

What about stage business chosen to enforce the Spine; do you determine that consciously or does it come intuitively?

I think it happens both ways.

As Shylock, you have a thing of wrapping yourself up in your gabardine, that obviously comes from the concept of protecting yourself.

The Group Theatre production of *Awake and Sing*, 1935.

The Group Theatre production of *Awake and Sing*, 1935.

Yes, I never thought of that. I didn't invent that thing consciously, but I can think of a semi-intellectual choice that at the same time has much emotion behind it from my work in *The Tempest*. As Prospero I endow Ariel with power. How do I do it? I can do it simply by thinking it. I can say, "Go, bring the rabble,/O'er whom I give thee power, here to this place." The words themselves carry the permission to use my power. But instead, it occurred to me one day to put the palm of my hand out and encounter his, not touching; only so as to convey my vibrations to him, so to speak. Well, that's a very legitimate piece of business, and as a matter of fact it peculiarly colors the whole audience's understanding of our relationship. They like it; and I like it, because it's true. Where did it come from: emotion? intellect? Both. Everything.

Does that relate to the idea of da Vinci?

Not necessarily, no. You can't make a Procrustes' bed of da Vinci's face, if you forgive the maladroitness. You can't fit everything into it. What I receive from da Vinci's portrait is just a kind of impulse which is started at the beginning of the play, and recurs in the course of the action from time to time. For example, that same scene in which I also give Miranda to Ferdinand. I might play it, if I chose, smilingly: "This is the day of betrothal, my children, be happy; I give you to each other and your troubles are now over; and understand, I do this for your own good." Well, I don't take it that way; that's one place where the reviewers might say, "Why don't you smile? You're giving your daughter away in marriage." I refuse to smile; because life is essentially tragic, that's why. In the scene, unconsciously, the face of da Vinci recurs to me. "How would he feel about it? What rights does that da Vinci face give me here?" And what I see is that, as Prospero, I am committed, as everyone is, to a lifetime of tragedy.

But you don't ask yourself that all through the play.

Oh, no. Only when I need it, Peter. After you are confident of your Spine and of all your adjustments to everything that happens, there's no reason you shouldn't simply respond to the current of the play. But there are certain moments in the play which need reinforcement from the Spine. One such moment is that great one, "Our revels now are ended." What would you say is the action behind the speech that follows? "These our actors,/As I foretold you, were all spirits, and/Are melted into air, into thin air:/And, like the baseless fabric of this vision,/The cloud-capped towers," and so on. What would you say should be the adjustment to that speech? The emotional adjustment?

Well, there are two things working: the Action to end the nuptial ceremony so that he can take care of the conspirators; and the adjustment of ending it peacefully without alarming the lovers and ruining their wedding.

I think there's something more. In a moment he's going to be saying "My old brain is troubled . . . a turn or two I'll walk,/To still my beating mind." "You go into the cell," I say. And they answer, "We wish your peace." Well, this is an indication, Shakespeare's indication, of the *nature* of that whole moment. Prospero is deeply troubled. He suddenly remembers that there is evil, there is ill brewing in the world; and you cannot turn your back on it. There it is. "I had forgot that foul conspiracy/Of the beast Caliban and his confederates/Against my life." It isn't only my life; it's every life as long as evil exists in the world; and here I have watched these two young lovers witnessing a beautiful ceremony; and I'm ruining it for them. I have to interrupt it. In this moment of "essential" thinking, he finds himself saying, "What can I tell them but the truth? Dear ones, despite all illusions to the contrary, there is nothing that survives; this is the world we live in. Believe me, you must do the best you can with it." As I expressed it the other day, "Be of good cheer, there is no hope." This is what he is saying. But "it is for you as a strong and loving young man, for the sake of my beloved daughter, who is 'the third of my own life' as I've said, to try to make a world in which this kind of hopelessness will be less effective."

Doesn't that make him rather negative?

On the contrary, I think it's very positive. What he says is: "Face up to the world. A beautiful apparition. That's the way it is."

You've changed your interpretation of Prospero. In the earlier lectures you said that Prospero's whole Action was a desire for revenge, changed by Ariel's saying, "If I were human, I would forgive them."

It still is. Prospero's purpose still is unchanged. But in a different direction. The channel is different. When at the end he says to the king "I am going to witness, I hope, the nuptial of our dear children, and after that 'retire me to my Milan where/Every third thought shall be my grave'." That's slightly different. "I'm willing to return, not in order to forgive and say everything is fine: 'my traitorous brother, you are all right, I've forgiven you'." No, that can never be really forgiven, but it's got to be faced up to.

Before, it seems to me you were saying that the main event of the play was a man's return to life; but it now appears you see the play more as a man's facing up to death—a man confronting himself with death.

Well, there it is in the play.

But aren't both things in the play?

It's not only the actual death, but facing up to the enemies of life. Whatever is inimical to life; which is a kind of death, death in life. So that what he expresses at the end is, "it's a bitter pill I've swallowed, I'm not going to have my revenge, even if there's a sweetness to that revenge. I refuse that. I will not degrade my human quality by going in for revenge."

That seems a much more mature, profound look at the play. Does that mean that the first time you did it, you had a different Spine?

Not a different Spine exactly, but it took a different direction at the end.

How then would you articulate your Spine for Prospero if it's not a striving for revenge?

Fundamentally, it's a striving for a better world; but in order to achieve it, it would seem that revenge comes first. "I'm going to get my own back." In this way he's something like Shylock. But then, when Imagination in the person of Ariel suggests, "it's a waste of life—revenge; all right, you'll do a little house cleaning, but to stain your human quality with an act of blood is beneath you, beneath a man's potential." This he accepts as his final philosophy: "I forgive, but in order to live in the world, I've got to return to it." That's the idea that holds the play together for me now, while before it was simply a very pleasant act of forgiveness followed by, "Here we go back, and I'll be restored; my child will have children, my grandchildren," and so on.

Despite my viewing of the play from a slightly different perspective, that moment with Ariel is still the high point that I was talking about earlier: when Ariel says, "I would, if I were human." By the way, I don't think that Shakespeare has given me as Prospero enough time to make that transition. That's a very rough moment to make. I have to pause and take in what he said; and one must be very careful when the play is coming to an end not to pause without real significance. That pause is a dangerous one. There's not enough buildup to "I would if I were human." When Ariel says, "Your charm so strongly works 'em,/That if you now beheld them your affections/Would become tender." And I as Prospero answer, "Dost thou think so, spirit?" To which he replies, "Mine would, if I were human." "And mine shall . . . " that is a fairy tale ending if ever I heard one, how to provide the psychological background for that repentance? Suddenly, complete change. "And mine shall." "What you can do, Ariel, I can do." Prospero forgives, although there is evidence that the two main villains are unrepentant, another bitterness in his cup. He forgives but they're not to be forgiven, really.

I perceive the real richness and maturity of The Tempest. *If this play is taken as Shakespeare's final statement, ("I'll drown my book") what he's done here is drawn and summarized from all his periods of writing. In a sense Sebastian and Antonio are that expression of his* Measure for Measure *period in which evil exists and evil will inevitably continue to exist.*

Yes, I think that's right.

Earlier you used the term "actor's scholarship." What do you think is different about studying a play for an English class or for a lecture on Shakespeare and taking a script, say Hamlet *or* Lear, *and studying it for playing a role or the role?*

Well, the crucial thing is, of course, that the actor has got to perform the play. His problems are perhaps even more demanding than those of the scholar. The scholar, who comes to the play as something to be studied and grappled with in his own study, observes the usual amenities with regard to a script: when it was written, the artistry with which it was written, the historical significance, and so on. This is all very important; there's no limit to what an actor can learn or study; but this general enrichment, in my opinion, has little to do with the actual work of planning the play or the role. Yes, it fertilizes the actor's mind to learn as much about the script as possible. After that what takes place is the *act of choice*, the act of weeding out and choosing that which is important to the play as a dramatic object, as an artistic product.

How do you weed out what you can use and what you can't?

By relating, I think, to the way the dramatist has responded to the historical material which he's been given. Shakespeare himself must have excised; he must have chosen what he wanted out of the enormous material that was offered him. It enriches the actor's mechanism to have as much knowledge and detail as he can of the period or the background of the play. It's a major aid toward understanding the style of the play, but even that is not going to help the actor to act the part, so what does he do? He begins to examine the play from the point of view of his own necessity for playing the role, in conjunction with the other actors who also have that necessity.

And what's the first step?

He starts from the basis of actuality. I often say to my students, "Whom are you playing?" and they will answer, "I'm Juliet." or "I'm Mercutio." and I say, "No, you're not." They're puzzled for a moment, and then they get the idea; they realize what I'm saying is, "You're Jane" or "You're Henry" or whoever; in other words, you're yourself. Now you begin to study the play from the point of view of *your own* talking and acting out the actions of the play. Once that's realized, you're, at any rate, off on a real foot, and not attempting to grasp the whole period and the whole character all at once.

The first reading is always very important, and it should be utilized—I'm not counting the previous readings which have taken place at home in every actor's case—as the first realization of one's own simple Self in contact for the first time with the other Selves of the cast (I'm now calling it a cast rather than a play), of realizing that it is precious at the first reading to *connect* with the other person, to have him connect with you, and to begin to make discoveries. It's the actor's job to continue to make discoveries, always, as I stress so often, in the search for the fundamental thing, the essence, the Spine which is eventually going to determine everything in his character. Now that's a general all-around statement of the approach.

I think the process of rehearsal is the history of the finding of ourSelves. We begin with ourselves, which is why a first reading is usually pretty good. And then we begin to lose ourselves; we grapple with other material in the play, sometimes profound, sometimes superficial. Finally, at the end, when it's all amalgamated, and everything is in place, it's then that the Self rises and says, "I am here." In order to grasp the Reality of the plays, I find myself automatically asking, "Who are these people? What are they here for? What are they doing? What is the essence of their relationship to each other? What's it all about?" Michael Chekhov once said, "Examine the relationships of the characters." Lear with Goneril is different from Lear with Cordelia, different from Lear with Gloucester. Edmund-and-Goneril is a different thing from Edmund-and-Regan. Kent with Lear is a different thing from Kent with the Fool. All these things begin to be examined in the course of rehearsal. That first reading isn't going to be perfect, but it's all important, because it allows people to look at each other really and find out about each other, even as fellow actors.

What about reading the play prior to the first rehearsal? How do you undertake that?

The reading of a play is not a dry, scholarly, obedient thing. No. Especially the reading of a play like, say, *A Midsummer Night's Dream*, is an act of falling in love. You are almost immediately seized by the extraordinary qualities of the play; and that means you are already, whether you know it or not, brought in-to the atmosphere of the play. You perceive that the characters have certain connections with each other which are expressed in divine language. You fall in love with the divinity of that language. You fall in love with the sheer act of creation by the crew of mechanicals, led by Quince and Bottom. Your knowledge of the play and your recognition of it, for recognition is an act of love, extend and expand further and further until it includes the whole world of the play, until you cannot think of Bottom without thinking of Theseus; you can't think of Quince without thinking of Puck; and so on. It all belongs together. If you say no more than, "My God, I love this play!" that statement of criticism is really an act of mingling with the material of the play, which is invaluable to the actor before he even opens his mouth. In that particular period of approaching the play, the actor will be like Bottom who wants to do all the parts. He'll say, "My God, what I can do with this, what I could do with that!" A man might even be attracted to playing the women's parts. It doesn't matter. He loves them all; and that is a degree to the kind of excitement, the real love for the play, which is important to bring to the first group reading.

The other day I had the experience of reading a play that I had never read before. At the first reading what I found was that I was attracted by the style of the author. What do I mean by that? In this case by his desire to say something new, original, and true about the material of the play. This was enough to make me want to read it twice. Sometimes I throw a new play down after reading no more than a third of it. But here I read it through. Now, the second time I read, I was already acquainted with the quality of the various characters, and I began to pick out certain places where I said again, "Gee, I'd like to play that; or I'd like to play *that*," without knowing what my own part is, but nevertheless I'm "creatively" drawn into the material of the play, so that if I were suddenly to be informed that I was going to play the lead in this play and come to a first rehearsal with that experience behind me, I would have that much more of a grip on the style of the play, not only its actions which have to be thoroughly sifted and examined in the course of rehearsal, but the whole feeling of it. Is it satirical? Is it ironic? Is it poetic? Is it just plain real—realistic?

After the first reading, do you come to subsequent rehearsals with a preconcieved plan of work?

You might, but you shouldn't commit yourself to final answers at the beginning. You should allow yourself to make more and more discoveries. If the play is rich enough to have impressed you with its worth, its quality; well, then you can be sure that there are many things to discover which you didn't find at the first reading. And so especially the first rehearsal, and I believe the first several rehearsals should be devoted to examining and trying to find the simple verisimilitudes of the play—the way people relate to each other, the way they talk to each other, the way people wear their clothes even, it's not too early to begin to imagine that.

To imagine that? I've worked with actors who actually wear costumes to the early rehearsals.

I don't think you have to wear any special costume, although I believe costume is intended to, and it does, help; it's the—a phrase I'm very fond of—it's "the outside of the inside." Just as *mise en scene* is the outside of the *content* which is the inside of the play.

Doesn't it bother you to have to imagine all these things: to play with imaginary swords and have to play with imaginary robes, and then also to have to relate to the truth of the circumstances? Doesn't that get in your way?

Why should it? The imagination, which is the guide of all these things, is capable of taking you to the moon every bit as well as the rockets that we're using now, and even further. We're way ahead of the astronauts in that respect.

You have mentioned Shakespearean critics such as Goddard and Harbage. How valuable do you find them; and how do you find them valuable in the preparation of a role?

Sometimes they're basically valuable. Goddard was very instrumental in forming my own final acceptance of an approach to the character of Shylock. Goddard, as I found, happens to have been a Quaker, and his whole moral attitude toward life and human activity was committed to the Quaker view. I'm not a Quaker and I don't know very much about Quakerism, although I'm aware it is dedicated to good works and a humanistic view of the world. Goddard then, in approaching the material of Shakespeare, said in essence: "Either these people are real, or I'm not interested. Shakespeare wrote them; and he made them real. He made them to be like human beings all over the world: like you, like me. In that case, recognizing that my own belief, the very cornerstone of it, is based upon a faith in the amelioration, the possible betterment of mankind, I cannot but choose to believe that this was also Shakespeare's faith in this enormous body of humane writing that he did." Therefore, the logic continues, "I conclude that since Shakespeare's basic belief is that man is good and desires to be good, man will desire to *do* the right thing in the world which he has inherited. Even the evil, which is delineated in some of the characters, produces a kind of pain in those same characters which I believe is the result of being frustrated in the desire to achieve their full humanity." Now that could sound vaguely sentimental to some people. They might immediately protest, "Do you mean to say that Iago and Edmund and Richard III are in any way repentant because they were not able to do the right, the holy thing in this life?" And I would have to say, "Obviously not, because of their behavior and particularly of the way their lives end, but I would also add in line with what Goddard thinks, that the Unconscious is a mighty, hidden thing below the surface, and who knows what it was that inclined Iago or Edmund or Richard III in the path they took?"

But is that relevant in terms of the events of the play? It's interesting that this conclusion came to you while working on Shylock, because of what you said about The Merchant of Venice *being about the corruption by money. It seems to me that Good in the play doesn't triumph at all at the end—that Portia is just as spoiled a girl at the end of the play as she was at the beginning, that Bassanio is just as much a fortune hunter as he was at the beginning of the play; Antonio is also unregenerate.*

Antonio is lost. The fact that Good is overcome and defeated in any condition, and especially the conditions of a significant play, doesn't mean the Good does not exist. The monumental example of this is *Lear*. Even though the play ends in dire tragedy, there is a great Nevertheless: nevertheless, there was this Cordelia; nevertheless, there was the Fool; nevertheless, there was Kent; nevertheless, there was Lear himself.

But Lear learns. Who learns anything in The Merchant of Venice?

We learn. And I believe the path is cleared for some of the characters to achieve insight as well. In my understanding of the play, thanks to Goddard and his suggestions, a Portia is not exactly "richly left," to misuse Bassanio's phrase. In my feeling, after the end of the play, she is going to find out that her Bassanio was, from the beginning, little more than a fortune hunter, that all his airs and graces when it comes down to considering the manhood, the *worth* of a man like that, come to very, very little. Then perhaps in her brooding; because I think that she has a mind which disposes her to brood and to contemplate, to think over the past: the significance of life, the future, and so on; she may be led to the conclusion that "that man Shylock: that man whom we ground under and caught between the millstones of the law; that man had something, no matter whether he was wrongheaded or not, he had a quality, a human entity and an essence which far surpasses anything that I have ever met in any other person." That to me is the residue of the play. Shylock himself may die as a result of his defeat, nevertheless he has "fought the good fight," and in a peculiar way, he has overcome.

All these things reside, I think, within the responsibility of the director. That's why, by the way, in no production of *Merchant* that I've been in, have we really, basically succeeded. We've straddled the fence. We've given you both the horrors of prejudice and persecution on the one hand, and the saving grace of sweetness and light and poetry on the other.

Isn't that implicit in the play? The Romantic atmosphere in that play is so very strong.

It is indeed, but in my belief we mustn't succumb to it. I've nothing against the Romantic view. No matter what you do, *The Merchant of Venice* is for us a Romantic play, if for no other reason perhaps than that the people wear different clothes and reflect life in Romantic terms. But a better word to use as the basis of every play of Shakespeare's is Reality. Behind this Romanticism there is a very stern, sometimes even ugly, Reality.

What about the language, which seems to militate against your interpretation? Do you perhaps see the language itself as an embarrassment of riches, a corruption?

That's pretty well spoken. That could be right. It indicates a totally different approach to the play and perhaps other parts of Shakespeare. Because moonlight and roses are spread all over that last scene—"In such a night" and all that other charming, lovely poetry, why should we take it for granted that Shakespeare meant this to be a kind of absolutism of all evil? Tackling it the other way, perhaps it is possible to assume that in "the dark backward and abysm" of Shakespeare's mind was something like this: "Well, these people do return to their original Belmont life; they do utter sweet nothings; they do croon over each other and go to bed and are obviously and trivially happy over the joke of the ring in the last scene. But—*who cares?* What kind of nonsense is this? Can this atone for all the evil that exists in the world: for prejudice, for anti-Semitism, and for the fact that one human being has been ground down and out?"

You're saying essentially that in Shakespeare as in life good words don't have to necessarily betoken good people.

It strikes me that perhaps the preservation of the contradiction in human behavior is the profoundest business of the director in dealing with a play like this, and perhaps with all the plays of Shakespeare,—not necessarily to take even Shakespeare's people at their face value. Before Shakespeare's time, as you know, the Morality plays of the day simply assigned one quality to a character, and he was known as "Obedience" or "Virtue" or "Chastity" or "Lechery" or whatever. Shakespeare is far more complicated than that.

How do you play that? How do you play that fact that what people say is not necessarily what people are? You say it's the director's province, but if you were Lorenzo in that particular scene, how would you go about playing against the atmosphere of moonlight and roses?

Well, I saw a very interesting example, apropos Lorenzo and Antonio, in London last summer during the National Theatre's production of *The Merchant of Venice*. In the last scene the director injected an idea which made the ending of the play most revealing. Lorenzo in this production had already lost the fire of his passion for Jessica; while she, a renegade to her Father and her people as we know, was given the deed to all of Shylock's property by Portia. She stood there holding this paper while Lorenzo, although he's delighted by the receipt of the money ("You drop manna in the way/Of starved people," he says), leaves her. He goes off somewhere, and apparently abandons her to her own resources. He's bored with her. Possibly a case of "all passion spent." As for Antonio, the director had him linger there out of a kind of curious fellow feeling for Jessica who is the last person left on the stage; and in a wordless confusion, he looks at her, she looks at him, she looks at the deed in her hand, and then he drifts off all by himself, and she's left there at the end. That's partly an answer to your question. It can be done, but it requires, as all things do in the theatre, the cooperation of actor and director. I still hope that someday this production will be done, in a completely unified way, supporting the idea, which I state again: Gold is the villain, and the theme of the play is the corruption that stems from money, from wealth. Some day, from beginning to end, from the moment Antonio says, "In sooth, I know not why I am so sad," right down to the end with the exit of Antonio, I'm hoping that this idea will permeate the whole production of the play.

You mentioned before what happens to the characters after the play is over. Is it part of "actor's scholarship" to determine what happened to the characters before the play began? Obviously to some extent that's true because of what you said about Ben Stark in the Odets play, but his past is referred to in the play. Do you ever, in terms of your own actor's scholarship, try to go through what Stanislavsky calls "a flow of the day"—what the character does from the moment he gets up in the morning to the moment he walks through the door for his first entrance?

Stanislavsky has given us many attractive, sometimes brilliant, examples of that kind of thing, and of course, I accept the possibility of it; but I do think one can find a short cut in this regard. If we take our cue from Portia, for example, in *The Merchant of Venice*; her first words, note, are, "By my troth, Nerissa, my little body is aweary of this great world," in which she seems to echo Antonio's sadness. Well, what does she do with herself for the whole livelong day? It is certainly worthwhile examining this question. We find her lazily proposing to Nerissa that she, Nerissa, pronounce the various names of the suitors who have come to ask for Portia's hand, and she will then exercise her wits at their expense. Well, in a way this is a lazy rich woman's caprice—one way of passing the time. I assume before that she's risen and yawned, eaten a luxurious breakfast, had the hairdressers in, and lazily occupied herself with various activities until this moment. But these are all hunches and notions of the imagination. If they help to give an atmosphere to the part of Portia which stems from the idea of the laziness of gold, the laziness of unused property, the laziness of having inherited so much wealth that there is no need to lift her finger to do anything about it; perhaps they are of value. These things are actor's choices, always together with the director, if he wishes. Anything that will stimulate the imagination is good, but I think one should not wander too far from the material of the play. I think that once one realizes what the *function* of the character is, in light of his Spine or his Main Action, one should stick fairly closely to home base. The play itself assures the audience of that which needs to be filled in, and also encourages the audience to use its own imagination; so that while I would agree that the actor can greatly deepen his work on a character he is playing by being very specific about that character's biography, this can be carried too far. If however, somewhere along the way of examining "the flow of the day," as you say, one comes up with a central detail; this may, as I think I demonstrated with the part of Shylock, determine the course for the whole character. Of course, the mightiest example of this is King Lear. What freight shall Lear carry with him into the first scene? We don't know who he is. Here he comes up the steps, as we played him; he sits on the throne and the first thing he says is, "Attend the Lords of France and Burgundy, Gloucester." Gloucester goes off. And then Lear says, "Meantime we shall express our darker purpose." And the play begins. From what primary purpose antedating his first entrance do his subsequent actions flow? That's a question for a whole new discussion.

Are there any other examples of how you found the central stimulus for your character?

Oh, yes. I'll give you an example out of *Twelfth Night*. I played Feste at one time. There's something about the whole part of Feste, the quality of wit and humor, which is devil-may-care. It's loose and free. It says, "I don't care whose toes I step on. Let them whip me, as they did when I was younger, I don't care, I just don't care." At his first entrance Maria reproaches him. She says in effect, "Where the hell have you been? Olivia, our lady, has been calling for you. Where have you been?" And this was for me "Spinal." It gave me a sense of his having wandered carelessly,—maybe in the fields, maybe with some girl into some bordello, who knows where, but he'd been wandering. And as a matter of fact in the course of the play he does just that. He wanders to Orsino's house and sings for him. It doesn't matter; so long as people fling him a little money, he's happy. He doesn't give a damn, except in one regard. He resents being stepped on by people whom he considers to be his intellectual inferiors, for example, Malvolio. Well, this is just about all you have to know about the position of Feste in the play. Along the way you learn that he has a special kind of charming love for Olivia. She's sweet; she lets him alone; and she doesn't raise too much fuss when he disappears. In a sense he's a miniature kind of Falstaff, because he loves life and he loves the expressiveness of other characters who love life, such as Sir Toby and even Sir Andrew. He's like the expression, "fancy-free" or "Thought is free." He's untrammeled; there's no rope attached to him. Although he's a hanger-on at Olivia's house, he wanders, and that wandering quality is the central point. It doesn't matter about his dramatic destiny, to use two heavy words, because he doesn't figure that way in the play.

But he *is* related to its overall theme, which is perhaps to be found in some such expression as Sir Toby's challenge to Malvolio: "Dost thou think, because thou art virtuous, there shall be no more cakes and ale?" Perhaps the whole idea of *Twelfth Night* is contained in that little nugget. This is for the director to decide, but it's somewhere in that locality. There's where I would look for it. Why? Because in reading the play I am attracted by that quality in all the characters. Those who go against it: Malvolio, Olivia herself to some extent, Orsino to some extent, simply prove the validity of those who are for it, who are on the side of that theme.

By contrast, I once stated the central quality of *As You Like It*, perhaps even its theme, in three words: "green, gold, goodness." Where that came from I don't know, possibly my unconscious, but "green" suggests the quality of the forest; "gold" the quality of human character and also perhaps the social stratum that the play is set in; and "goodness" in the whole character of the controlling goodness of all the people. Goodness as such, without being regarded too narrowly as moral, morality, but just plain good, the goodness of life. "Under the greenwood tree/Who loves to lie with me,/And tune his merry note/Unto the sweet bird's throat."

In *Twelfth Night*, however; although the feelings of the two plays are related; there's a certain sadness. I think it's imparted by the pervasive quality of Viola's character, which might be expressed in the statement, "She never told her love,/But let concealment, like a worm i' the bud,/Feed on her damask cheek: She pined in thought . . ." To "pine in thought." Well, *Twelfth Night*, as you know, comes just before *Hamlet* in the canon, and one is tempted to believe that Shakespeare himself was pining a little in thought, and preparing for his own more sober and serious period.

Isn't there also a sadness and autumnal quality in Feste?

Yes, there is, and his song at the end of the play expresses it: "When that I was and a little tiny boy,/With a hey, ho, and the wind and the rain,/A foolish thing was but a toy,/For the rain it raineth every day." Yes, it's the coming of rain.

Perhaps it's also the coming of winter: Twelfth Night, *the twelfth night of Christmas.*

I don't know. I don't think that the title describes what the material of the play is. I think it simply says here's an entertainment written for you to be performed on the twelfth night of Christmas, make of it "what you will." I venture to think it reflects Shakespeare's point of view at the time, the whole mood of his life.

So, there you have it; when you asked me about actor's scholarship at the outset, I can only answer you by saying it consists of reading the play, absorbing the play, reading it again and again and again until you find something that takes you by the hand and says, "Here—this may be of help to you." This has been my experience certainly in *Merchant of Venice* with Shylock, and as I've said, with Feste, certainly with Lear, and of course, Prospero,—in every part.

When sculptors work on stone, they perceive the object within the stone. It's there. There's nothing intellectual about it. It's emotional. It's a kind of magnetism which says, "Come to me" or in another way, "Extricate me. Bring me out of my prison. I'm here. I'm waiting. Come and get me." Well, in the same way, the choice of Spine is imbedded in the play, not according to this critic's understanding or that director's interpretation, but *yours* and yours alone, so that my own choice is one that belongs to *me*. You may agree to such an extent that *you* accept it, and you may find it feeds your whole creative mechanism. That's all right. But that's the way we should think about this matter of choice. We don't say, "Now let me see, what shall I choose?" No. The choice in a sense makes itself.

It becomes an inevitability according to what you are looking for. I assure you that in the case of Shylock—to use that because it's a perfect example in many ways,—when I came across this line which said, "You spit upon my Jewish gabardine" something in me said, "Wait. Hold on there. Stop." And later: "You that did void your rheum upon my beard." Surely that is the source of the indignation which is contained in this one speech; but let's see, let's see, does this indignation amplify itself? Has the stone fallen in the pond and are the ripples spreading to include and perhaps engulf the whole play? Yes, every time we see him, the same thing is activating him. Every time. Even in bidding farewell to Jessica, he says, "Lock up my doors . . . Let not the sound of shallow foppery enter/My sober house." The necessity to protect his own integrity, the integrity of his house, of his daughter and of his religion.

We were talking about Prospero earlier and the fact that your view of the role had matured but the Spine had not changed. Is there any case where you found the Spine of a play and years later repeated your performance and discovered a completely different Spine?

Not that different, Peter. In the case of a part, say, like Lear there wasn't a lot to change; there was nothing to change about the whole approach to the part. It had been worked out and examined so carefully in the beginning that it remained substantially the same at the very end. But I played it in Los Angeles a couple of years after I had originally played it here in Connecticut; and there—I simply take it from people who saw it both places,—they said it had become deeper and richer. I'm glad it did, and the only reason that I can possibly find is that in two years maybe I had matured a little bit myself with relation to the part and its issues, the play and its issues. Certainly this is what happened more consciously in the case of Prospero. When I first played it, I was content to allow the play to say that this is Prospero's or Shakespeare's reconciliation with the world. Now this world of ours today had gone through one hell of a clash, tremendous cataclysmic changes. Not only did my world survive, but perhaps for Shakespeare, as I conceive, his world had survived the same kind of changes. One has only to think of his world, beginning with *Hamlet*, *Othello*, *Macbeth*, and *Lear*, particularly, not to speak of *Troilus and Cressida* and *Timon of Athens*, to perceive that there was a time when Shakespeare's mind had been colored by the waste and violence of this particular period of his life. And we see that in his last plays a more mellow point of view seems to prevail. Well, that mellowness was, I think, what our first production of *Tempest* aimed at, and which at the time I was very pleased to accept. I liked the idea of vengeance, colored gradually by imagination and hope, exchanging its aims for those of peace, tranquillity, and forgiveness. I still like it. It's a nice idea; but in the light of the life we lead now, I think our view of Shakespeare's work becomes altered. And even after this short period of eleven years I say to myself: Prospero, and behind him Shakespeare of course, is too much of a Realist to pretend that now everything is going to be fine and dandy, that he's returning to a life which is going to reflect all of the original innocence of the Garden of Eden, that's nonsense. Life goes on in its complexity and its recalcitrance.

I think I had more hope eleven years ago. We've gone through so many upheavals, and the war which is still going on has persisted for too long for anyone to believe that human intelligence is working (as it should). Our lives are full of hatred and suspicion. Even when a person does good, we ask, "What's the motive?" Does this commit us to the thought of a final conflict which is just beyond all thought? So we're plunged into a bitter reality, which we can't escape from, and we might as well say, "That's the way things are," and somewhere in the back of our minds, hope that it will be better for our children.

So finally, though you don't think that that's necessarily right for the play, it's right for the time. If you did Prospero again in another eleven years, and the world situation were much rosier, you might interpret the play in a third way.

I might. I don't know. I might. Of course there are other positive side issues in *The Tempest* which are every bit as fascinating as the main issue itself. One of them is contained in that great speech, "Ye elves of hills, brooks, standing lakes and groves." It's a happy act of the imagination for me, while saying that speech, to remember that Shakespeare himself is incorporated into this last character of Prospero and that when he comes to this speech, what he's really expressing is a final statement of gratitude to the forces of Nature which have made him what he is both as Prospero and, to my mind, much more as Shakespeare; because the recurrence of natural detail, natural themes, natural objects all through Shakespeare's work just can't be overlooked. It's organic with everything he writes; and so when he comes to this farewell, what he's say-ing is, "I have achieved certain things in my life, and I owe it all to little powerless objects in my youth, in my childhood, who have guided my whole way of life." "By whose aid, weak masters though ye be." He has previously mentioned a few of them, you elves who make the mushrooms at night, you elves that make the fairy rings at night, you elves that seem to dance along the shore and recede as the waves come in to chase you, and so on. Well, all of these things have helped me to write my plays, and what are they? The tempest itself, "I have bedimm'd/The noontide sun, call'd forth the mutinous winds,/And 'twixt the green sea and azured vault/Set roaring war." *The Tempest.* "To the dread rattling thunder/Have I given fire, and rifted Jove's stout oak." Who is that? *Lear.* I've rifted him "with his own bolt." "The strong based promontory/Have I made shake." *Othello.* "And by the spurs plucked up/The pine and cedar." *Macbeth.* "Graves at my command/Have waked their sleepers." *Hamlet.* "Oped, and let 'em forth/By my so potent art." These things I have done literally, but, much more important, figuratively in my plays. "But this rough magic/I here abjure." Rough in two senses. It's been pretty rough writing these plays. "And when I have required some heavenly music," and so on. "I'll break my staff." I'll resign from this way of life, and I'm going back. I'm going back. It affects me as I do it, but I'm sure that the audience can't possibly get it. It thrills me to think that I have played Lear, that I might play Macbeth or Othello.

When you do the speech for me that way now, it opens up whole new worlds. But do you think about that when you do it on stage?

I do. Yes, I do. That for me is the kernel, the "grain" as Stanislavsky calls it, of the speech. That's what it's all about. And I can't possibly convey it to an au-dience; I don't see how anyone could.

And yet it doesn't have anything to do with the magic cloak or the island or anything else. It's completely outside that.

Not necessarily. The magic cloak is art, is talent. Ariel is imagination itself. The last act of the play is "Farewell, Ariel. I'm dismissing you, too. I've no longer any use for you. I love you, and I'll always remember you, and I'm grateful to you, but goodbye. Goodbye."

Rocket to the Moon, 1938.
Eleanor Lynn and Morris Carnovsky.

The Group Theatre production of
Night Music, 1940.
Morris Carnovsky and Jane Wyatt.

The Group Theatre production of
Thunder Rock, 1939.

The Group Theatre production of *Paradise Lost*, 1935. Morris Carnovsky and Stella Adler.

The Group Theatre production of *Rocket to the Moon*, 1938.
L. to r.: Eleanor Lynn, Morris Carnovsky, Ruth Nelson.

Characterization

How would you define characterization?

Well, roughly, characterization is the actor's response to the image that has been given him to create. In so doing, he presents certain aspects of himself in order to flesh out the portrait. It never really departs from himself. You can't provide the author with an image which is dissimilar from something in you.

All of us, I believe, are capable of everything. We have inside ourselves all the extremes of emotion and desire; and it is that capacity that I think the actor brings, in the last analysis, to the making of his part. That's the Self.

This does not necessarily mean that just because you seek to find yourself in every part, everything you play will issue in exactly the same way. Alfred Lunt, for example, was a very sensitive and responsive person on the stage; and of course he had his mannerisms, his qualities and eccentricities even, but that didn't stop his imagination from working.

You once told me that you really aren't right for Falstaff, that you would only give it a good reading. But that didn't really appear to be true when you finally performed it. It was very, very good. What do you mean by a good reading if you say that everybody is capable of everything?

There is always a penumbra where the actor overlaps the qualities that are required for a part but doesn't exactly fit them. I can understand the actions of a Falstaff, especially in relation to his Spine which we had talked so much about. But, while I thoroughly enjoy the physicalization of a Falstaff, the fact is that I am wearing padding and like the frog of the fable, I am endeavoring to be an elephant. I am not fat in actuality so I must rely on being fat in imagination; and as long as this "muscle" of the imagination is capable of working, it has the strength to hoist me onto the level that I require. Nevertheless, in the case of a part like Falstaff, there might always be a desire on the part of some in the audience to say, "I wish he had been a little fatter, a little bit more naturally 'juicy,' a little bit more sanguine in temperament and not quite so cerebral."

But are you advocating type casting then?

Not really. We used to say about Rudolph Schildkraut, who was the first great actor I ever actually met, that he could play a bathtub if he chose. Here was this small, almost gross-looking fat man, who was simply magnificent, world-shaking, when he'd step on the stage. But I don't think even if he had desired to play Hamlet that he should have; and I don't think he would have wanted to. There is a limit to what anybody ought to ask of himself. You wouldn't require a Sidney Greenstreet to do Romeo.

How then does type casting relate to the idea of Self?

All parts relate to the idea of Self. Type casting simply makes it easier for the director to direct and for the public to understand. The trouble with it in our system is that it is often apt to be a pursuit of qualities which are primarily saleable, commercial. You see it very well in Hollywood or on television. A person might want to play a part differently from the way he played it in his last picture or his last series, but the director will say to him, "No, we want you just as you were. We want *only* that. We're not interested in that other idea that you have." That's a kind of occlusion to the growth of the actor. He wants to expand, and depending on what he wants to expand, his talent or his pocket, a decision is made for him then and there.

Types become, as Harold Clurman once observed, monsters, sometimes very charming monsters, but they exhibit a group of characteristics which limit them. If you stray outside the circle which is Cary Grant, you're not Cary Grant any more. Besides, there are one's notions of what one's career is. No doubt, for example, Cary Grant has had a marvelous career from the point of view of Hollywood, but I would still continue to wonder whether there isn't a little more to Cary Grant than we are permitted to see.

Has Hollywood thought of you that way?

I think they had a tendency to do so, yes. I was cast either as a good solid charming member of a community, fathers, etc.,—I played the father in the Gershwin film, *Rhapsody in Blue*; or diametrically, I was cast as villains and gangsters.

Like Edge of Darkness *vs.* Saigon.

Yes, that's the idea. And neither of those characterizations or denominations would have satisfied me in the long run. I'd have gone crazy if I'd simply had to stay in Hollywood playing parts like that. Also, as I said before, they put a kind of wall around your talent, around your desire to unfold. It would be impossible in Hollywood for me to think about doing Lear. But later when I had done it in the East and *then* went back to Hollywood and did it, that was all right. I was already "typed" as Lear.

Do you think there are two kinds of actors—the kind exemplified by Spencer Tracy on one hand, and the kind exemplified by Laurence Olivier or Paul Muni on the other?

There are differences. In Spencer Tracy's case you never expected him to be, you didn't want him to be, anything but Spencer Tracy. The precious thing that he had to convey was the kind of "Tracyism" that we remember. Muni had a different way of approaching the Self; and I don't think it's necessary to compare one with the other to the detriment of either one. Muni had the need to create a kind of exterior physical image, along the line, perhaps, of that described by Coquelin; and after he created it, something in himself, Paul Muni, nobody else, responded and filled that image. It was as if he made the outside first and then entered into it completely. I think that there was more to Muni than he ever showed, and the conditions of our theatre and our movies, which I have just been speaking of, made it necessary for him to stick with a kind of flimsy account of himself, thin, watered-down.

With Tracy, you had the unadulterated Self always working in a way that was not only acceptable, but very agreeable, so that the impression you got was of Spencer Tracy constantly. *There* was an actor for whom it was perfectly right that he should be the recognizable Spencer Tracy. But does this mean that Muni or Olivier (and I think I may count myself in that category) are exhausted by the doing of one part? We may always, in the last analysis, bring our full sensibilities to the manufacture, so to speak, of a role. But that Self that we bring to it is a constantly changing, and perhaps enriching thing.

When you play characters who are more remote from you physically, how do you work on those external characteristics and still maintain a sense of Self?

You have to plan for it, simply to organize your body in a different way, just as I had to learn to live with my padding when I did Falstaff. There is something about exterior physical characteristics which is very stimulating to the actor's imagination. An actor can look in the mirror (I've done this), see himself, see his make-up, and see that it is good. You may observe that your costume is well-styled and that it hangs on you very well; and you get a sense of completeness from that. This idea extends to extremes as well: like the figure of a hunchback or adiposity or whatever; and that being so, the Self lends itself almost immediately to the image so that finally it is not terribly different from the ordinary Self that you use in other non-extreme, more normal parts. I think a mistake that's made is to torture the voice, for example, when a young, inexperienced actor plays an old man. It's not necessary; the image does it for you. There is something in your Self that responds to that image if you let it. It isn't that you go on as usual just playing in your ordinary voice and using your ordinary gestures . . .

. . . but something will rise to the padding.

That's right. I think that this is a result not only of experience, but of faith, faith in your physical qualities, and it comes from the brain, from thought. I was illustrating the other day to an actor who is about to do Malvolio at Stratford. He was asking me some questions about the role, which I myself had played some time ago in San Diego, and he said, "I don't know how to hold myself in the part." I told him, "Don't think about that; just try to establish the nature of Malvolio, the fundamental nature of a man of that kind *through his eyes*, first. Let your eyes say for you what you think of all the characters on the stage: a certain kind of superiority to the couriers around Olivia, certainly a sense of superiority, even dislike, extending to Feste the jester, and even toward Olivia herself. Certainly the respect of an inferior toward your 'boss,' but colored by a shade of contempt for her encouragement of these other lesser people. And you'll find then that from the very act of looking at people in that manner, you may hold yourself differently; you may manipulate the staff that you carry in a certain way; you may finger the chain around your neck; you may turn your head from right to left in a special way. And that, becoming more physical as it does, will induce a general psychological attitude in your whole body. So that when you come to the climax in the counterfeit letter Scene, where this image attempts to fortify itself into greatness—'Some are born great, etc.' it overreaches itself and the image falls to pieces at the end where you say, 'I will do everything that thou wilt have me.' " This is the unusual Malvolio, almost frantic with the desire to please. I suggested to him that he will discover these things physically at first out of his relationship to the implied circumstances, the Objects, and the people on the stage.

The whole sense of Shylock as a "beleagured wolf" which we discussed before is something which, if the actor lets himself alone, will infiltrate and fill his whole body as well as the mechanism of his thinking. So that he may find his whole attitude toward all the Objects which he encounters in the manner of a wolf who is being attacked or surrounded. But it also even invades the area of speaking: the voice becomes different, the rhythms that suggest themselves become different; all this happens spontaneously.

It's not as difficult as it may seem. One of the best ways of encouraging it is the knowledge of your body in terms of centers as Michael Chekhov has pointed out. You find that you are capable of placing the center of your power, so to speak, in any area of your body that you choose. For example, the actor playing a person who is given to thinking a great deal might place his center automatically in the center of his head, and everything about his body would follow suit; the head would take sovereignty over everything else in his body. The inventions might then become riveted through his eyes and through his voice. A favorite example of Michael Chekhov's is that of a highly inquisitive, prying, nosy person. There the center might be posted in the very tip of his nose and would thereby engage all of his activities in a physical way. His body and his mind would be focused on a desire to find out, to probe; and as a result you would have a unique kind of character. In the case of Sir Toby Belch or Falstaff himself, you could place the imaginary center in the middle of your belly, and you will find, after practicing it for a while, that that same center would give off rebounding rays to the rest of your body and to your mind so that your stomach would seem to be the leader in all the activities of the body, controlling and regulating all of your functions: the use of your hands, your feet, the way you sit, the way you look at Objects, the way you turn around so as to circumnavigate your own girth, and certainly your voice, its rhythm, the way the words come out in measured fashion. These are things that you don't think out; they happen automatically because you have chosen this center for all your being, stimulating your imagination to shape your activities.

I once played Doctor Caius, the French zany, in *Merry Wives of Windsor*. I imagined that he fancied himself quite a man with the ladies, also a terrific swordsman. He was nothing of the sort, but he thought he was. He has great vanity but it's all unfounded, all in his head. I think I automatically placed the center for him in the area of my eyebrows so that, in my imagination, that part of my head behaved as if it had wings and would lift me off the ground wherever I moved. The noteworthy thing about the placement is, as I've said before, that the rest of the body *falls in with it*.

Peter Quince in *A Midsummer Night's Dream* is another case in point of prompting physical adjustments through the specific use of the imagination. This is a darling character; and his charm lies in the fact that he wants to do the best possible job of play producing for the sake of a man whom he admires very much, that great gentleman Theseus, and for the sake of Theseus' marriage to Hippolyta. Quince's whole body is full of that anxiety to be good; and as I do it now to demonstrate, I find that it lends a particularly naive feeling to my eyes which are seeking for the correct way of doing the play that the Athenian mechanicals are trying to present: the lines have to be said correctly—these lines which he himself perhaps has written; the actors have to come in on the right cues, and so forth. He cares about his job and therefore physically he's immersed in the script. And this immersion takes a kind of physical form which gives the actor's body all of the characterization that it needs. It may influence his walk. The actor may choose to be a trifle nearsighted. Trembling with nervousness, he may use his hands in a certain way, pointing out that such-and-such is wrong, and such-and-such is right. All this, as we discussed earlier, is developed from his desire to please Theseus and Hippolyta by creating something beautiful for them. After finding the activities by which that Action is expressed, all that is necessary is to apply the right make-up which will carry out and put a kind of seal on this activity; and there you are, there is Quince.

Did you find that in working on Falstaff?

Yes, especially in rehearsal and before rehearsal. The feet and the legs would be deployed in a certain way but always they were carrying the center which is in the shape of a belly. Of course, I can't deny that I was filled out by padding. It helped enormously. Also the look, the sheer physical look—the made-up look of a face. You come down from the dressing room; on the way to the stage you encounter a mirror; you look at it, and if it presents your own hoped for image, it encourages you to continue the life of that image and take it onto the stage with you. It's almost as if in the first phase of rehearsal you ask, "How should I make him look?" Some very good actors will ask the director on the very first day, "What do I wear, what do you want me to look like?" Because the image is something which is very conducive. It invites the actor to merge with it. I prefer to think that the actor makes his own image. He objectifies the thing; he sees it in front of him; then he takes it; he absorbs it into himself. In order to do this, of course, he's got to recognize and accept the Spine of the part. That first moment of encountering a character is all-important. And all-inclusive; suggesting not only ideas for the way you look—that's the final seal—but also what you are inside, directing your search for what you are and do—in fact all the things that we've been talking about.

You could base your character on pictures. Say you're looking for someone in the Renaissance or the post-Renaissance era. In examining certain portraits you might come across one that seems to be the very thing. You study it, and you might be seized by one aspect of that picture as I was by that self-portrait of da Vinci while I was preparing the role of Prospero. You might say, "Yes, that's it, that look in the eyes. Yes, that's what I want." You may not, nor need to, approximate that same look in the eye because actually nobody can look precisely like anybody else. But you have an inner urge in that direction, and that's the urge to characterization. Then in that moment you realize that there is only one way that you can respond to the image, only one. For example, the portrait of Richard the Third at the National Portrait Gallery in London tells me a surprising lot about him. There is a kind of tragic, haunted look in that face. And the fact that he's putting a ring on his finger may be the foreshadowing of the placing of the crown on his head. A sensitive man about whose death at the end we might say as Octavius says about Brutus that under other circumstances he might have been a great man. Or as Fortinbras says about Hamlet, ". . . he was likely, had he been put on,/To have proved most royally." (That by the way is the residue of any tragedy: "My God, if things had turned out otherwise, what this man would have been, what this woman would have become.")

There is a thin but well-defined line, I think, between the producing of a "characterization" and the simple playing of a character. For example, for Ben Stark, that character in *Rocket to the Moon*, all I actually needed was the suggestion of the wall between me and the world to induce in me a certain quality of yearning which applied to the whole play within its proper circumstances. Outside of that I played myself. "I" plus that predominant quality was no longer "I" but the character. And I hesitate to call that a characterization although it certainly took that direction. Characterization is required when your character has well defined physical characteristics—perhaps on the verge of eccentricity. It's roughly similar to the old doctrine of the humours in Shakespeare's day. Incidentally, it's very stimulating to the imagination to allocate such fundamental qualities to characters, asking yourself to what degree these various elements are mixed in their behavior. Earth, Air, Fire, and Water. You can practically describe so many of Shakespeare's characters in terms of these qualities. A Mercutio comes under the "sign" of Fire; Richard the Second's might be water; the Gravedigger in *Hamlet* or even Falstaff are Earth; Jacques in *As You Like It* could be Air. You can mix these ingredients in any way you choose.

Take, for example, a character like Polonius; in a certain way he is a little bit like a Danish Dr. Caius because he imagines himself to be much more sagacious than he really is. On the other hand, he has a certain rough and ready wisdom which comes from his dealing with men in a difficult position, namely the Court. He's chief counsellor to the King and respected as such, and so you have to assess to what degree your water and gasoline are going to mix. I recall very distinctly in the case of playing Polonius, whatever inner qualities I had chosen for him endowed my presence on the stage with a certain physical consistency. I had to be just as alive and foolish in the scene where I give my son that sage advice as I am in those scenes where Polonius excites Hamlet's contempt and satire.

There are numerous characters in Shakespeare that, from a physical point of view, require no more than your habitual Self. A character like Henry V need be little more than the person who is properly chosen to play him, physically able to impress with the looks of a Henry V. This lies in the domain of casting. In addition he should, of course, be able to realize what that Self of his is required to do within the given circumstances. For a young man playing Henry V to be a warrior, sit on his horse, and direct the activities of the battlefield, these come under the heading of circumstances. They don't require the actor to change his physicality in any way. To wander about the English camp at night incognito, sitting and talking to the soldiers, again doesn't require anything more than the simple man chosen for the part within those circumstances. There is very little demand for what we call characterization in a humorous scene like the wooing of Princess Katherine of France. It is still fundamentally the actor who is chosen to play Henry V in the circumstances of the character.

Even a part like Iago need not require particular characterization. The actor playing him is called upon to exert a kind of mental influence, not only on Othello, but on the audience, so that he appears to be what Othello calls him, "honest Iago," the embodiment of a sinister intention masked by complete openness and honesty. There the characterization, if you like, is an inner one. It comes from the understanding of the complete Action of Iago. No great demand is made of a physical change as far as he is concerned. The actor naturally may choose to do something of a private and personal nature. Iago for example knows how to drink and he knows how to summon others to drink so that the actor may choose certain physical qualities which are suggested by that idea, characteristic gestures, similar to the one you remember my doing as Schweyk, that habitual salute, but it's not essential. What is basically important, however, is how the actor will serve the character. You can call it characterization, but it doesn't go much beyond the presentation of the person chosen to do the part. That doesn't mean to say that the actor chosen to do the part *is* an Iago, but he certainly must understand what Iago is all about.

What about the danger of turning a characterization into a caricature? And how do you handle plays which seem to function on two levels of reality, for example, Henry IV, Part One *with its Hal and its Bardolph?*

They're different in degree, perhaps, but not in fundamental reality of nature. The actor playing Bardolph, as well as the actor of Hal, is going to have to summon his own Self, his own reality, in the midst of this exterior which he has legitimately placed upon himself and which may even go in the direction of caricature. The fundamental requirement of everything is reality. You ask how can one escape turning an extreme characterization into a caricature? Some plays require that you do just that, but the reality of Bardolph is that he's a sodden drinker who has absolutely nothing to recommend him except that he lends himself to good clean fun, like robbing travelers, and for the rest, drinking himself into an impossible condition; and who is, for some reason, encouraged as a companion by the man who is eventually going to be King Henry V. But note—there is a certain distorted, crooked kind of love for Falstaff in this Bardolph simply because Falstaff does encourage him to be a member of his company. What is the last word that Bardolph has about the death of Falstaff? "Would I were with him, wheresom'er he is either in heaven or in hell." That's the remark of a very sensitive and really charming character. So if the actor playing Bardolph were tempted to go beyond the needs of the play and become what you call a caricature, he would have to be reminded of the fact that "you're the man who is going to say, 'Would I were with him, wheresome'er he is.' "

You mentioned that the costume can give you that final touch which caps the character and your work on it. Has it ever happened that you haven't found the role until you've put the make-up on?

In a way it has. You may have found it, but there's a special, almost triumphal arch put on it when you see yourself in your costume and you say, "Yes, that's it." The very opposite may happen too. You may put your costume on and feel betrayed. That's happened to me. There was a production of *Hamlet* some years ago in which I played Claudius. I felt that there was no proper bridge of understanding between the costume designer and myself. He was a good designer, and it was a good costume—but not for me. Then there was another occasion out in Hollywood when a wonderful designer did the costumes for *Lear* and presented me with one of the most exquisite sketches for the mad scene when Lear comes in crowned with flowers. It was not only spiritual, it was *spirituél*. It was almost bodiless. It was a fantasy of the costumer's imagination, utterly beautiful, but I could not play the scene that way. It stymied me from beginning to end. It would require my whole body, my make-up, everything to be readapted to a new situation. It was an idea of the designer but utterly wrong from the point of view of the production. Yes—the costume is very much a part of the characterization.

Do you think ideally that the actor should be included in the first planning stages of a production?

Ideally, yes. Perhaps not in the first planning stage, but certainly I think his ideas, and his secret, if he has one about his sense of a certain part, should be shared with the costume designer; and if the designer has the right kind of sensitiveness and imagination, perhaps then a perfect result might emerge. In many ways, as far as I was concerned, the most perfect costumes in Shakespeare that I've ever had in a really big part were those of the original Lear that I did. They were not what you would call the usual Stonehenge-influenced costumes, but somehow or other they let the actor alone. They helped the actor to act.

As I talk about this matter of characterization which seems to dwell in the main on physical characteristics, usually regarded as superficial, I must remind you and myself constantly that *within* this image which the actor in a way imposes on his being, there remains the Self that we've been talking about ever since we began this dialogue. This it is which gives life, not only to the physical characteristics, but to the costume itself. It's almost as if when everything is ready, everything absolutely logical and replete, illuminations are turned on which radiate from within, from the Self of the Actor.

In a larger sense, the character of the play itself is like an actor's costume. Now the all-over costume, so to speak, of a *Macbeth* is different from the all-over costume of a *Hamlet*. Maybe this is a convenient way of thinking about the difference of styles between plays. Go over it in your mind and ask yourself what the dominant look, the visual appeal, of an *Othello* is. What is that rich Venetian clothing of a story like that of *Othello*? Compare the Venice of *Othello* with the city of *The Merchant of Venice*. I'm not only talking about the costumes of the people. I'm referring to the atmosphere of those plays. Compare for a moment the atmosphere of *Merry Wives* with that of *Twelfth Night*. Or *Twelfth Night* with *As You Like It*. Fundamentally, the actor approaching characters in these plays produces as real a result in both cases, but one is adapted to a certain type of atmosphere and the other to a totally different one.

Let's take Jacques in *As You Like It*. Compare him at random with Kent in *King Lear*. The actor who plays Jacques one week might well be cast as Kent the next. What's going to be the difference between his approach to one play and his approach to the other? They're both going to come from the same shop; the same man is going to be doing both parts, but obviously in *As You Like It*, the Jacques is going to have to call on somewhat different qualities in himself, qualities of devil-may-care cynicism, of a feeling of superiority; and yet as the actor who is going to play Kent he will have to simplify his nature, throw out the cynicism, substitute loyalty and humility, love. And all these individual character discoveries and choices must be adjusted to and tempered by the over-all atmosphere of the play as determined by the director. A Jacques grafted into the Kent scenes of *King Lear* would be very much out of place. There would be no function for him. He'd be an excrescence.

My intelligence will guide me to the first acceptance of the play as either a realistic play, a tragic play, a comic play, a fanciful play, or a clownish play. One of these categories will suggest itself to me. If it is an all-over clownish play, then my place in it is that of a clown. If it is an all-over realistic, tragic play, out with the clowning. There's no room for it. My address must be to the realistic circumstances of the work which I must try to understand and with which I must harmonize.

We call our book *The Actor's Eye*; and almost the first suggestion that comes to me when I think about the difference between these various categories is sensible to me through my own eye. The things I see (the way my eye behaves) as I think of a drama like Ibsen's *Ghosts* are quite different from what I experience when I think about a comedy like *Twelfth Night* or a play like *Merry Wives* or *Much Ado* or *Macbeth*. The eye here is truly the window of the soul, and for me an entrance way to the solution of what we call style. Style is like a dog that's always yapping at our heels, because here in America we almost never cope with it. All we know is that if you turn us loose in a play that is obviously realistic, well, you act as naturally and realistically as possible; that's your style and in a way that's true. But we American actors are not generally at home with Restoration plays for example. We're not to the manner born, although I think we could achieve it. But how?

First of all, we would have to come to grips with the manners, the modes of the period of the Restoration. We'd have to find out how to wear the clothes. We'd have to imaginatively transform ourselves into the people who would wear those clothes. We might be led to realize that manners mattered a great deal in that day, and that manners often masked a kind of brutality between men and women, that for all its finery and plumery, it was fundamentally a dirty kind of age. We would have to look for things to feed our imagination along this line.

And where would we look?

The usual places to begin with: books, museums, biographies; hear the music of the period; read, of course, the plays and novels of the period; be either enchanted or repelled by the historical records of the period. And again old Imagination would raise its hand and draw together all the elements that we could gather out of these sources. Then we *might* find the proper way, the perfect way, of stepping on the stage as Mirabell or Millamant. Don't you get the feeling when you read a play like *The Way of the World* that you are looking at some very strange animals by comparison with what we have today?

Michael Chekhov says the first thing to ask ourselves is "What is the difference between me and them? Between me and him?" Would he ever sit in the way I am sitting here? Would he arrange his body in a certain way? Would he have a look in his eye which has been generated by the cynical, almost contemptuous attitude of the day? Would the necessity for uttering wit at any cost give him a certain sense of lightness, of buoyancy, a bubbling quality? Would he choose his words in a totally different way from the way we do today? When he relaxes, is he aware of the fact that he forms a certain line with his body? And what does all this mean? When he thinks of the woman he's in love with, how is he going to engage her attention, how is he going to enchant her? How is his way of enchanting her going to be different from any way that we might employ? He wouldn't just send flowers or candy. There might be a formal ceremony about it all. He might send a carriage with, perhaps, a turbaned footman who would deliver a huge roomful of flowers with a witty note. All these things make for style and character. The source of them is life, the life of the day; and the more we are acquainted with that life, the better we are able to incorporate it. Which is why I imagine English actors consider themselves, and really are, much closer to an understanding of the kind of behavior that we call Restoration comedy, Comedy of Manners.

When I was exploring these things a few moments ago, and actually doing them for you, I was more or less suggesting the line along which I might think and try to model my behavior, but at any moment along the way I could have said, "I, Morris, am Joseph Surface;" and immediately it would change my "Morris quality" within the outer "Joseph Surface;" but always beneath Joseph Surface would be me.

In rehearsal for the American Shakespeare Festival production of
The Merchant of Venice, 1957.
Katharine Hepburn and Morris Carnovsky.

As Shylock in the American Shakespeare Festival production of
The Merchant of Venice.

The Use of the Soliloquy

> Now I am alone. (*Hamlet*, II,ii)
> I am myself alone. (*Henry VI, Part 3*, IV,vi)

It is said that Shakespeare's sonnet is the key for unlocking the poet's heart, and this could well be for the purpose of our understanding the emotions he experienced. Similarly the device that Shakespeare offers us actors for the study of his plays is the Soliloquy, for it's the Soliloquy that gives immediate and broad indications of the character's dominating Action. The Soliloquy may be thought of as an alembicated idea held in suspension with great intensity, with intense concentration of character and purpose.

This is almost painfully true in the case of, say, Macbeth, where the whole pressure of the imagination is intense enough to become almost self-punishment. In *Hamlet*, although the quality of Hamlet's thinking is utterly different from that of Macbeth, we can feel almost the same concentration.

To me, the most interesting and extraordinary element in Macbeth's character is not necessarily the fact that he is brought to the point of murdering a king, killing the guardians of Duncan's bed, smearing their faces with blood, and all that. This is the vision, of course, which haunts us in the play—perhaps the first thing that comes to our minds when we think of *Macbeth*. But the exciting thing about Macbeth, the really moving thing about him, is that he is a great *poet* and in moments of profound emotion, tremendous images are bodied forth. To incorporate that into a performance is to strengthen and to give quality to the Spine; so that Macbeth won't be just a man who is gratifying his ambition and his wife's ambition and who pays the piper for it at the end, but he will be this fascinating murderer-poet capable of a shuddering imagination. That is the character to be created on the stage; it transforms the whole play. It's as if the conscience of the world itself were violated and made sick by his act. "Thought sick" as Hamlet says.

Another illustration is Claudius in *Hamlet*. His great soliloquy in the prayer scene, "Oh my offense is rank, it smells to heaven," is the revelation of an extremely sensitive and conscience-ridden man, a man who in spite of his obvious abilities to control and to rule a kingdom is yet haggard and haunted by his one great mistake. A kind of miniature Macbeth, you might say, although there is nothing miniature about murder. He has killed, but he suffers in a different way from Macbeth. He suffers morally. Macbeth is haunted by the images which arise out of murder. Claudius really examines himself as a ruler, a capable ruler. He is haunted by the moral consequences of his deed because he feels, as other characters in Shakespeare have stated, that once you initiate crime, you may expect retribution: "This even-handed justice," as Macbeth calls it, is part of the very essence of life. Here is a man, Claudius, who suffers from the fact that he cannot repent. "I can make an effort to pray but the words won't come. I know what I utter is a pack of lies, that I am fundamentally corrupt; and that therefore

My words fly up, my thoughts remain below:
Words without thoughts never to heaven go.

That's not just a couplet to seal off the speech. It's a terribly self-incriminating and self-recognizing statement—a wrenching confession. So here is this man whom now we see as not just the drunkard of Hamlet's point of view; not just the lecherous lover, "his fingers paddling" in the queen's neck and all that. He is not just the cavalier and easy statesman he appears to be in his first scene. Here is a man who carries in his viscera the pain of his own terrible deed. And in the light of this soliloquy we will understand all that he has done from the beginning, up until this moment, and throughout every scene that follows.

One of the reasons for doing soliloquies in classwork is that the student actor is forced to find the Objects of his imagination. He is alone on stage and therefore he must relate to himself. It can readily be seen how this applies to any of Hamlet's soliloquies for he is constantly upbraiding himself, scolding himself, exhorting or examining himself. He is his own prime Object. But there are other Objects which the actor calls to his support in the course of a speech by Hamlet. The prime example of this kind of work may be found in "Oh, what a rogue and peasant slave am I." For the student actor this speech is especially important because it revolves around some very definite Objects: the Player-King, his dead father, the usurping Claudius, and himself. From the vantage point of his own Self all these other Objects are intensely called into life. As we've said, "the Object saveth from death," and in this case giveth enormous life. For Hamlet is, at this moment of soliloquy, in actual contact with these Objects, *physical* even though they are imaginary.

But the study of the Soliloquy isn't only a device that's intended for the student actor. It's one that serves the actual performer. Of course, in the case of

Hamlet, the actor is first compelled to grapple with the teasing question of all questions: "What makes Hamlet tick? What is his Spine?" Well, I have found a Spine for Hamlet that makes unifying sense for me; and as usual it comes about, as it did in this case, through constant reexamination of the play.

There's a scene in the play which normally doesn't strike anyone as more than simply another shadowy facet of the character; his fidelity, his feeling of trust, his feeling of humanity and brotherhood, love. Well, any scene that contains those basic qualities is well worth examining from the point of view of the search for the Spine.

It occurs just before the play within the play. Hamlet is alone with Horatio, and he suddenly finds himself saying, "Horatio, thou art e'en as just a man/as e'er my conversation coped withal," adding that he has found Horatio to be the perfectly balanced man and then he continues in almost a rhetorical mode of speech, "Give me that man/That is not passion's slave . . ." What the speech masks is a love for his life-long friend Horatio. But what is significant about it, and what I think it reveals, is Hamlet's deep awareness of the fact that a man may be required to do a number of things in his life which are against his nature. The ideal man is *he who resists any invasion of his own integrity.* "The soul has its majority," as Emily Dickinson has expressed it.

Hamlet's words indicate that a man is engaged in his profoundest work, his profoundest search, if he is seeking the truth about himself. Such a man will not even be swayed by the fact that a ghost has come to him and said, "Go, murder someone." Harold C. Goddard in analyzing Hamlet's character amplifies this point.

> For what was such a man made? Plainly for the ultimate things: for wonder, for curiosity and the pursuit of truth, for love, for creation—but first of all for freedom, the condition of the other four. He was made, that is, for religion and philosophy, for love and art, for liberty to "grow unto himself"—five forces that are the elemental enemies of Force.

And then he goes on to say,

> And this man is called upon to kill. It is almost as if Jesus had been asked to play the role of Napoleon (as the temptation in the wilderness suggests that in some sense he was). If Jesus had been, ought he to have accepted it? The absurdity of the question prompts the recording of the strangest of all the strange facts in the history of *Hamlet*: the fact, namely, that nearly all readers, commentators, and critics are agreed in thinking that it was Hamlet's duty to kill, that he ought indeed to have killed much sooner than he did. His delay, they say, was a weakness and disaster, entailing, as it did, many unintended deaths, including his own. He should have obeyed much earlier the Ghost's injunction to avenge his father's murder.*

*Goddard, Harold C., *The Meaning of Shakespeare.* Chicago, Illinois: The University of Chicago Press, 1951.

What I like to repeat for myself is the description of the essence of Hamlet: "For what was such a man made?" What was the reason? Why was he born? "Plainly for the ultimate things: for wonder, for curiosity and the pursuit of truth, for love, for creation—but first of all for freedom, the condition of the other four." *Hamlet* is an overwhelming study in the maintenance of man's integrity. "What a piece of work is man." Everything in *Hamlet*, wherever you put your finger, seems to point in this direction. This is what I see as the Spine of the character. Is the attempt to find yourSelf simply an intellectual pastime? Isn't it rather one of the greatest, most difficult tasks that any man can pursue? I am persuaded that Shakespeare must have felt it keen and in our own time Brecht asks, "What is a man?" It would seem to be the haunting necessity for all artists.

What is revealed then returning to this scene with Horatio is, in a moment of love and closeness, really the very essence of Hamlet's character. Such a man *cannot* brutally murder someone out of revenge, even though the world, society, everything that impinges on him, urges him to do so. Eventually when Hamlet does kill, it is in a moment of impulse, in passion, but not in cold blood. So—starting with this scene, if you agree that it contains a basic statement of Hamlet's character, you the actor then look for it to expand throughout and saturate the whole play. Your job is to test whether this is expressed from the first moment ("A little more than kin and less than kind") to the last ("The rest is silence"). If the actor is sufficiently a poet, he will make the connection between these three points—the beginning, the middle statement, and the end. Of course, I am not saying that this particular scene expresses the whole of Hamlet's character, there's plenty more where that came from; but it's one of the most significant moments in the play.

Viewing *Hamlet* from this perspective, "The rest is silence," would seem to suggest that you may want to be faithful to your own integrity, but humanly you are defeated; life defeats you in the long run. That's the tragedy of it. The production of *Hamlet* that I envisage would have that as its dominating idea.

Incidentally, the function of the actor playing Horatio, then, is to understand how Hamlet sees him. He must convey the kind of man "who is not passion's slave" as Hamlet says, who provides the reason for Hamlet suddenly measuring himself against Horatio almost as if he says, "We two are lonely; we're alone in this corrupt world. I'm glad you're there, and I would like to be a member of your society. We two against the whole world." I think if Horatio's function is understood in that light, the actor who plays him will have his choices defined throughout the play—a life of his own, nor merely a foil for the Prince. He will understand what his Action is; he will understand how he attains his own deep tragic awareness at the end when he catches Hamlet's body in his arms and lays it down on the ground.

This Spine, for me at any rate, answers the question that is always raised about Hamlet's madness and about his "inaction." In the moment of shock after the Ghost's revelation, it is not only Hamlet who is discombobulated, shaken from his moorings; it's the world. In that condition, with all society vibrating and shaking around him, I do believe that he becomes a little unbalanced. As a poet,—that is, a person of intense sensibilities—he is "inspired" by this strange idea of pretending to be mad. Since the world is out of joint, as he says, I might as well enter into its madness.

That central statement—"I will at all costs preserve my integrity as a man"—this is what Hamlet examines in one soliloquy after another.

In the very first one you have this statement of it: in paraphrase—"I don't know where I am! I don't know what kind of world I inhabit! It's suddenly corrupt, ugly, horrible. A person who has been close to me, my mother, I suddenly don't understand her—I find myself wishing that all of this too, too solid flesh would melt, thaw, and resolve itself into a dew. I wish I would die. Simply disappear."

"Oh, what a rogue and peasant slave am I." It is easy to understand that Hamlet almost lives in a *vertigo* of indignation rising from the challenge the Ghost has laid upon him. Here he is examining what he must personally *do* in order to come to the truth. (By the way, "the search for truth" has been named as the Spine of Hamlet's whole character and of the play.) "What is truth?" Well, perhaps this is another way of saying what I've been saying. Hamlet confesses to Ophelia, "I could accuse me of such things that it were better my mother had not borne me." He admits to evil qualities in himself, but the one quality that he cannot give up is that quality which *resists* evil, and therefore resists the horrible suggestions that come from this life or from the beyond. A soliloquy like "Oh, what a rogue" presents pretty much the same problem to any actor who does it from the point of view of *any* Spine that he may select; but all an actor need do, following the point of view I suggest, is to infiltrate that same search, that same connection with the Objects, and with the basic sense of Self as revealed in the scene with Horatio. That will transform it. It will become characterized in a special way: I venture to suggest, Hamlet's way.

Later "To be or not to be"—an examination of the last shred of the integrity of things. Ask nine out of ten people about this speech and they will tell you that Hamlet is contemplating suicide. But I discard that. For me it implies, "not only am I being tested, not only must I decide what I am and where I stand, and what I do, but it would seem that the whole world is engaged in this reckoning—everybody." My test becomes a measuring rod for the questing activity of the whole world. "To be or not to be, that is the question." The whole nature of action—"What is a man to do about a world which challenges a man's deepest honesty to the extent that I feel it is challenging mine?" Then the impotent conclusion, "And enterprises of great pith and moment/With this regard their currents turn awry,/And lose the name of action." And nothing gets done. It's almost as if Hamlet is saying, "Yes, I would desire to be a unified man, but then I do nothing. Does a person have to accept the fact that we do nothing in order to retain our integrity?" The search continues.

There are times when Shakespeare goes sailing off into some private ecstasy of his own, undisturbed by any notion of realism or verisimilitude—such as the description of Cleopatra's barge or Mercutio's Queen Mab speech. Such also is Gertrude's presumed "purple patch" of grief at the drowning of Ophelia. I say "presumed" because many have regarded it as an interruption in lyric terms to the main business of the play. It *is* that but perhaps the moment can supply us with something more than a deeply sentimental lamentation of bereavement—the key perhaps to some hidden relevance not only in the soul of Gertrude but in the very heart of the play.

I'm thinking of the task of the actress. How will she join this moment with all that has gone before and all that comes after? Is there a binding clue *in terms* of Action that lies waiting in the text, one that will afford a satisfactory justification of *all* of Gertrude's actions? A similar hint perhaps of the one I found for Shylock.

The questioning, supported by imagination, ranges among all the possibilities offered to the actor for choice. Choice and rejection. What has Shakespeare given us to accept or refuse?

To begin with, is Gertrude even tacitly guilty of complicity in the death of Hamlet's father? Impossible, replies the actress—Gertrude is weak, helplessly in love with Claudius, with an emotion responsive to his fatal attractiveness, a convivial shoulderer of the burdens of kingship in the absence of her husband; someone to lean on, a romantic figure, strong, diplomatic. Of the Claudius that Hamlet sees, the "king of shreds and patches," the "cutpurse of the realm," she has no hint; she simply accepts the smoothness accompanied by carnival nights and conviviality, of the regency that (mind you) she has bestowed upon her new husband. To the general corruption of the Court style she brings no comprehension—until, that is, her son breaks violently into her dream of perfection, and for the first time she sees "such black and grained spots as will not leave their tinct."

In the shock and confusion of this self-discovery, Gertrude might well exclaim "What in God's name is happening to us?"—her first divination of what is "rotten in the State of Denmark." The revelation of pervasive corruption in her world will stay with her to the end. This, in my interpretation, is what infiltrates between every line of the soliloquy we are discussing: "What in God's name is happening to us?"

These two lost women, the helpless Queen and Ophelia, the toy and tool of princes and politicians, having to go mad and die to achieve any significance—their destinies conjoined in a "purple patch" that I have never seen justified either in critical comment or in the acting of it in the theatre.

How will the justification be achieved—for it must be granted that in the last analysis the answer must be left to the playwright, whose eye must be assumed to have ranged through every moment of these tragic destinies? If *this* particular moment is true, can it be construed as a link in the continuous and inevitable chain of a play called *Hamlet* where theme revolves around a society sick with corruption?

Admittedly Gertrude is a "twilight" figure, but in the functional climate of a play there are no "twilight" figures. Let me state boldly what I believe happens to her and how I believe she responds to what happens in the working out of her fate.

She diminishes as an individual. She becomes insecure, especially in her marital life. After the terrible scene with Hamlet in her bedchamber, I think she becomes permanently disoriented. She never finds the answer to her nagging question until the very end; with the one exception of her brave defense of her husband, she becomes a dim, lonely figure. It would be quite to be expected that she resorts to the solace of drink!

I must explain this last observation, taking responsibility for a conclusion that is nothing more nor less than a hazard of the imagination, nevertheless one that wraps up in a kind of unity the whole trajectory of the "wretched Queen." Can we discern a curious change in Gertrude's behavior in her last scene—a headstrong quality, careless, even loose; in the unbridled jocosity of "he's fat and scant of breath . . . the Queen carouses" and the four words "I *will*, my lord" that (for me) mirror the abandonment of a nature that welcomes its tragic doom?

This is the opportunity that beckons the actress to a solution that goes far beyond simple melodrama to one that evokes deep compassion and terror.

Each of Hamlet's soliloquies is fed by the compulsion, which typically any sensitive man has, toward self-examination, but each one is differentiated by the circumstances. Take the speech following Fortinbras's passing by with his army, "How all occasions do inform against me." This really states what Hamlet is up against. In a world of corruption where direct action is held up as an ideal, he finds himself an orphan. "Everything proclaims that I am useless as far as this world is concerned; and yet I cannot do otherwise. I may say that from now on my actions will be bloody, 'or be nothing worth,' but nothing is going to happen because I don't fundamentally believe it. I don't believe in shedding blood." So off he goes to England and comes back, and nothing has changed; and he dies, foolishly, in a sense.

To my mind, this interpretation goes far to explain the reasons for Hamlet's hold on our affections. He may do cruel things, nevertheless we identify with the motive behind his actions. Am I going too far if I say that if every person lives in order to achieve his own full Self, he recognizes in Hamlet that "there but for the grace of God go I?" Shakespeare through Hamlet, I believe, is presenting human nature at its most uncompromising. It may seem a relief that Fortinbras comes on at the end of the play, that Horatio offers to explain what happened so that the world will then get back on an even keel, but in fact life continues to make terrible demands and good pepole are always being called upon to set them right, "Oh, cursed spite."

The conflict between one's inner will and the world's demands leads to introspection. The Soliloquy, then, is a kind of jet of self-examination or of emotion. In acting terms it's the point at which the given circumstances collide with the actor's Will and the character's Spine. The Soliloquy comes then as an attempt to sort it out.

****

Perhaps an even more concrete example of the use of the Soliloquy occurs in *Romeo and Juliet*. The great Soliloquy for Juliet is, of course, the one in which she is about to take the Friar's potion. It is a greatly revealing speech,—the final test of Juliet's character. Life and death. She stands at the brink; she doesn't know what faces her; she has doubts about whether the good Friar is as good as all that. She overcomes those doubts. The thing that fundamentally agitates her being is, of course, her love for Romeo. She knows for herself that any solution that deprives her of her love is death; and she deliberately enters into a kind of living death. In the course of this soliloquy what happens is simply that as a person, as an individual, as a poet, as a lover, but most of all as a woman, she faces facts: she is confronted with a reality that arouses and excites her imagination in an inordinate degree. With the result that she actually *creates* all the Objects she imagines: the tomb, the corpses; she smells the smell of death. She sees and hears things: actually mandrakes torn up by their roots, howls, shrieks, and finally the visible apparition of her dead cousin, Tybalt, who flies across the screen of her imagination, sword in hand, to kill Romeo. This is her call to action. She confronts death and says "You will not have dominion over my love and I warrant this. I seal this statement by taking the potion."

So that you can see that Juliet's soliloquy in itself contains all of the ingredients not only of character, of personal essence, behavior, everything, but also of Action. There again a great soliloquy, a soaring moment,—important, central—becomes the pinnacle of the character. When you see Juliet coming in for the first time in the play she is a playful, even romping girl; but she has in herself the possibilities of this great moment, as I've described it. So that the whole progress of the play is conditioned by the fact in the actress's mind. As far as technique is concerned, it's almost as if the actress says to herself: "Where am I going? I'm heading toward that moment where I take the potion and cry, 'Romeo, this do I drink to thee.' " That in a way expresses the entire play and certainly the entire character. So that when we first see her, she already has within her the *capacity* of attaining that fatal certainty. There's a different look in the eye of an actress who knows that "eventually I am going to cry out to Romeo 'this do I drink to thee.' " A different look in the eye of an actress who knows that the whole experience of playing Juliet is going to be a celebration of undying love, an assertion that love never expires even though the lovers do.

How can the personal imagination of the actor not be stirred by such an idea? It's as if suddenly the world of Shakespeare becomes an extraordinary place which reveals its mysteries and possibilities, rousing the enthusiasm and the energies of the actor. Hamlet's "Oh, what a rogue and peasant slave" and this soliloquy of Juliet's, because they are perfect examples of the application of our "formula"—Self-Object-Action—are two of the most important soliloquies for the student to examine and perform. Indeed, there is no reason why, from the point of view of our work, a woman cannot do Hamlet and a man, Juliet.

****

By the way, when I say Soliloquy, I don't mean only the "Now I am alone" kind of soliloquy that Hamlet speaks. Sometimes a soliloquy may be a long speech as in the case of Hermione's address to the court in *Winter's Tale*. There you have a magnificent revelation of the very essence of a woman in Hermione. To my students I say, "If you were to take this whole speech, deeply touching as it is; and, after having recognized the human and moving nature of it, ask yourself how would you express this whole soliloquy, all of it, in a few words, what would you say?" I'm bending them to try to find the irreducible essence of the speech. Hermione is facing her husband who has accused her of adultery. Her whole nature is simplified, ironed out, refined through suffering. Words are almost superfluous. How then, I ask them, would you express the whole burden of that speech which is so illuminating of Hermione's character? What I'm searching for, what the students eventually find, is a very simple expression. Three words. "How could you?" Which amplified means: "With all our love, with all of our history of happiness together, in the light of everything that we've meant to each other, *how is it possible* that you could think such a thing of me and not only that, but callously expose me to the eyes of the world as well? *How could you?*" In their very simplicity, these three words, I maintain, bear the weight of one of the most tragic questions that a woman can ask a man. "How could you?" Sentimental? I am not concerned. The question vibrates with the anguish of a woman who has been wronged, of all women who have been wronged.

Here we have another example of a soliloquy that works backward and forward. This is the same Hermione whom we saw in the first scene, without guile, giving herself gladly to the moment, which is misconstrued completely by her husband; and it is this same Hermione who will eventually appear as a frozen statue, you might say, of wronged love. From the beginning to end, then, climaxing in this moment in the courtroom, she is one unified harmonious character.

These soliloquies are high points, climactic; essential points which mark the trajectory of each character. For the actress, the distillation of Hermione's speech into three words is useful because it has power to awaken the actress' emotions and thereby ours as we witness this terrible scene. Hermione's speech has style. She is a queen, trained from early on to express herself in noble terms, simple statements; even in this most wrenching moment of her life she expresses herself like a queen.

****

In the chapter on Imagination I mentioned Theseus in *A Midsummer Night's Dream*. Here is a character who is nowhere nearly as developed in the play as the obvious characters: the Bottoms, the Oberons, and the rest. And yet to make him as complete and consistent as the Hamlets and the Hermiones, one has to find an emotional and intellectual basis for this man. Well, is it not to be found in that speech about imagination: "The lunatic, the lover, and the poet are of imagination all compact?" It is a charming speech and a very true observation upon the nature of imagination. Why did Shakespeare give it to Theseus? One usually sees Theseus dressed as a warrior, the lover of Hippolyta; he conquered the Amazons and took Hippolyta as his bride. But in the play, actually he is nothing of the sort. He is an Elizabethan gentleman. Even though he is a ruler and subject to the harsh realities of his position, he has the sensibilities of a gentleman. An Elizabethan gentleman was responsive to poetry; in fact, as we know, some of them very often were sonneteers. And so, while I've never played Theseus, nevertheless I would, at his first entrance, make myself aware of the fact that this is the man who in the last act is going to say, "the lunatic, the lover, and the poet are of imagination all compact." The statement indicates quite an understanding of the nature of imagination. It reveals the quality of his mind and may also reveal the reason why Hippolyta can possibly be in love with him. In addition, he is even-tempered; he is moderate; a ruler but he understands the simple impulses in simple people. It is he who says in effect, "Let's not make fun of these mechanicals; they are giving us everything from the heart. They are giving us what they know, what they have. It comes to us as a gift." All these things add up to "gentleman" in the literal understanding of the word. He is the perfect moderator: his Action in fact may be described as "to moderate everything." But he does it with style. He is the complete gentleman in that he is also a great sportsman. He loves his hounds, for example; he loves nature. Certainly all very English.

Theseus talks of lovers and madmen having "such seething brains,/Such *shaping* fantasies, that apprehend more than cool reason ever comprehends." The word "shaping" is a very exact way in which to think about Shakespeare's own demands on the actor. Think again of the Object, the mental Object, as in Hamlet's "my father, methinks I see my father." That's not a cerebral idea of "father"; it involves Hamlet's whole personality, his relationship with the world. His father gave him a reason for being; his father was a *shaping* ideal, one that suggests Hamlet's own approach to life, that integrity we were talking about earlier. And a Soliloquy as an indicator of some kind of climactic moment can be thought of as the *shaper* of all of the impulses and actions that lead up to that high point of the play itself and lead away from it to the end. In simple words, the actor is active; he's not only a thinker. He's not only a feeler, but he acts all the time. He is making; he is shaping; he is molding. I think this is one of the reasons why Michael Chekhov used to lay such stress on the actor's "molding"; not only by the use of the hands as he outlines in his exercises, but molding by the *hands of the mind*, so to speak.

There's one speech that will, I think, shed some more light on the matter of the progression of the character; and that's "The Quality of Mercy" in *Merchant of Venice*. I've never seen it done from the point of view that I would like to suggest here. It's usually a bunch of violets thrust at the audience, a kind of purple patch which they all recognize and which seems to enclose some very flowery sentiments that you can applaud:

> But mercy is above such sceptred sway;
> It is enthroned in the hearts of kings,

and all that. One must ask, however, where does it come from? Portia doesn't talk like that anywhere else in the play. She puts on the disguise of a lawyer and comes to this extraordinary occasion in which a friend of her husband is being threatened by the knife of an Oriental, an outsider, a Jew. And suddenly she finds herself actually confronting this man with her view of moral values, such as mercy and justice. These two ideas, of course, are embedded in her address, but the human collision is what is usually absent. What is the Action behind the Quality of Mercy speech? And in what way will it again rebound backwards and forwards? How will it change and affect Portia at the beginning and Portia at the end of the play? Following upon all of the casket business, the high-flown sentiments, and everything that has developed between her and Bassanio, she discovers herself in the courtroom, in a very dangerous position. She pronounces, rather flatfootedly, "Then must the Jew be merciful." Suddenly she's face to face with a man who demands, "On what compusion must I?" Which is to say, "Who says so, what says so, why do I have to be merciful? Who the hell tells you to tell me to be merciful?" This, as I see it, shocks Portia, perhaps for the first time in her life. And she replies in effect, "Are you actually saying that you don't recognize the importance of being merciful to another human being? Is the whole idea of mercy cut out of your understanding of life? Why, you poor man. I'm sorry for you. You are astonishing." And in the light of this she speaks the speech which then becomes illuminated perhaps in some way equivalent to Juliet's soliloquy in the potion scene. Suddenly, she begins to make images, which is not altogether characteristic of Portia:

> The quality of mercy is not strain'd,
> It droppeth as the gentle rain from heaven

Upon the place beneath; it is twice blest;
It blesseth him that gives, and him that takes;

That is—"You've *got* to have mercy, man. I'm sorry for you if you don't understand that." In my opinion she becomes transfigured: enlightened and enrap-
tured. So that when Shylock turns his back on her and "calls for justice," it is, I
feel, a very transforming moment, in this Portia's life. Even though there's a lot
of trivial frippery that follows—the exchange of the rings and all that
business—there is left in her, I feel, for she is sensitive, a residue of "I have been
through an experience the like of which I never imagined could happen." I am
not really sure there's an actress in the world who could convey that. Parenthetically, I do believe that Portia is not going to continue to find her romantic
ideal in Bassanio. I dare to think that she has discovered her sense of reality
from this tragic scene in the courtroom. The sight of Shylock being ground up
in front of her eyes in the name of the Justice which she herself has precipitated
is something that she will never forget. We can give her that much credit, for I
don't think she is one of the colder Gentiles. And in the light of that, perhaps
there are other discoveries to be made about the beginning of the play as far as
she's concerned. Maybe something in her is waiting to be illuminated and
awakened. Through the very act of pointing out to an apparently inhuman
person the necessity to be human, she becomes humanized herself.

Many people would disagree with this as a rather fanciful interpretation.
They persist, as we discussed earlier, in regarding *Merchant* as a Romantic
play—Christian love balanced against non-Christian hate and cold-
ness. But I feel in Portia that there is a little sadness in her at the end. Perhaps
for the first time she recognizes that the reason for her opening words, "By my
troth, Nerissa, my little body is aweary of this great world," was that there was
something unfulfilled about her from the start, just as there was something unfulfilled about Antonio when he says, "In sooth, I know not why I am so sad."
Portia is one of the deeper people in the play; the deepest aside from Shylock. I
think this courtroom scene represents the education of Portia. She becomes a
person. She's married to Bassanio; she will be a good wife, but when she says,

How far that little candle throws his beams!
So shines a good deed in a naughty world.

perhaps there is a realization via her encounter with Shylock about that seemingly uncharacteristic statement of hers at the beginning. She has been capable
of wit, at other people's expense; she has been capable of a kind of gorgeous giving quality in her relationship with Bassanio, but suddenly her humanity has
been tested by this courtroom scene. Now I don't know how the actress can
make that transition, but I suggest that that is *the* challenge for whoever plays
Portia. To make it more difficult, *The Merchant of Venice* does indeed suggest a
very Romantic looking play. It is loaded with the ingredients of love and

laughter, a fairytale, exotic princes, an heiress, gold of Colchis and friendship seems to be a dominant theme throughout. The very names—Venice, Belmont—all would seem to invite a Romantic solution.

Furthermore, Shakespeare, for a man of his Age, would seem committed to show Shylock as an inheritor of the Barrabas tradition of Marlowe's *The Jew of Malta*. But Shakespeare was one of his kind in the whole history of the world; he was intensely human himself. Something in his makeup couldn't allow Shylock to be the sinister, unforgiving, and unforgivable person that many people would like to think he is or was. Something in him was for justice for the Jew, justice for everyone. And so I think that subconsciously (in our jargon) he was able to give Portia this opportunity to find her own basic quality. So I believe.

****

In speaking a soliloquy, the character, in a certain sense, is talking to a partner in his thinking. It's as if he is saying, "What shall I do? What do *you* think I should do?" That very process by which he fixes the "you" that he is addressing is the degree to which he creates the "magic circle" of concentration. For myself, I always try to relate to the Objects mentioned in the speech; I don't stray from the play. Or perhaps I might relate to some sort of alter ego—myself extroverted, so to speak—so that although I'm talking to myself, I am at the same time objectifying myself. When we talk to ourselves as most of us do, we usually make no sound, we think it through. But in the case of an Iago, say, thinking through his intended villainy, he is speaking to an alter ego who appreciates his scheming, who perhaps joins him in laughter, in the passion of his intended actions. And by supplying himself with an Object like that, the actor increases the activity of that *shaping* we were talking about, so that the moment remains packed with conflict, struggle. Another person is involved, even though that other person is himself, the projection of himself.

In summary, the Soliloquy, or even long speeches (like that of Hermione) help to reveal the most profound inner nature of the character. Let me repeat my earlier statement—soliloquies represent an alembicated idea held in suspension with a greater intensity than the dialogue which precedes or follows; through them you may discover the distillation, essence, or as Stanislavsky calls it, the "grain" of the role.

The American Shakespeare Festival production of *Hamlet*, 1958.
Morris Carnovsky and Geraldine Fitzgerald.

The American Shakespeare Festival production of *The Tempest*, 1960.
Joyce Ebert and Morris Carnovsky.

The Eye of the Storm: *King Lear*

> Meantime we shall express our darker purpose.
>
> (I,i)
>
> Who is it that can tell me who I am?
>
> (I,iv)
>
> Pour on: I will endure.
>
> (III,iv)

I was out on the road in San Francisco with a Noel Coward play when Joseph Verner Reed at Stratford called me up and said, "We're talking about doing *Lear* and we'd like to have you do it." I wasn't exactly flabbergasted because there had been talk about it before, but this time it was definite. I knew I was in for a terrific experience and I didn't know in advance if I could come up with all the solutions. Practically everything in *Lear* is an onslaught. You know you are in for a tremendous fight.

I got a copy of *King Lear* in paperback; it has a beautiful introduction by Alfred Harbage.* I read the play again and shortly after, Alan Fletcher, who was to direct, came out to see me. We sat together and I remember a kind of curious speechlessness between us. Suddenly we both burst out laughing and I said to him, "We're going to do it, aren't we?" He answered, "Yes, we are." And I said, "In that case we go for broke, don't we?" And he said, "We go for broke." That almost became our slogan. Knowing that we had to have great courage to tackle this play in the first place, we accepted the fact that no holds were barred. This was to be an all-out explosion, a giving of everything that we had. We certainly weren't the first ones to recognize that this was a terribly difficult venture. I believe that it was Peter Brook, before directing his version of

---

*Shakespeare, William. *The Tragedy of King Lear*. Baltimore, Maryland: Penguin Books, 1958.

the play, who compared doing *Lear* to climbing a high mountain, along which were strewn the bones and skulls of many predecessors. Well, we felt pretty much the same way.

In doing a part like Shylock or Prospero you have intervals of relative quiet; for example, Shylock's farewell scene with Jessica or even the comparatively calm reasoning first scene between Shylock and Antonio. That is restful compared to anything in Lear. Lear is a storm, in constant agitation, while the moments of agitation in Shylock are fairly few, powerful as they are. Since there's no saving of yourself, you've got to be prepared in playing Lear, not only for the part but for the whole play. For instance, the blinding of Gloucester, a fearful and violent scene. You must prepare for it in advance, facing up to the horror of it, the tearing out of a man's eyes. That act in itself is a mark of the necessity of seeing, and it must be presented for what it is.

Curiously, in retrospect, and as so often in the playing of Shakespeare, I can say that Lear was, in a sense, shaped before I came to it by certain things that occurred on my previous encounters with the play. One of the most formative of them happened when I was in college. A very fine teacher of mine brought a copy of *King Lear* into class. He announced, "I am going to read to you the scene of Lear's awakening, the reunion with Cordelia, when he awakes from his insanity." He read the scene and came to Cordelia's speech, "Mine enemy's dog,/Though he had bit me, should have stood that night/Against my fire." He suddenly stopped; sweat broke out on his brow; and he couldn't go on. He seemed struck dumb, and all he could bring out was the one word, "dreadful, dreadful, dreadful." I've never forgotten that. It foreshadowed completely the whole atmosphere of the play, and this before I attempted to discover its logic and its eventual clarities; but that single word "dreadful" has probably unconsciously dominated my whole approach to the play. I recognize in it the day-to-day collision of Man with his ultimate tragedy which is (let's, together with Shakespeare, face it) that of enduring and succumbing to the dreadful facts of existence and eventually dying without any particular promise of hope.

And even now, having played Lear, I can't bring myself to agree with those critics, among them Bradley, Barker, and Goddard himself, who believed that in the last moment of Lear in his reunion with Cordelia in death, there *is* a moment of hope, a moment of final illumination. I'm sorry but I see no such glimmer there. For me the picture is a bleak one and somehow or other the whole experience of Lear, of the writing of Lear, and the living through of Lear as Shakespeare must have done, is to me the reflection of a bleak moment, a bleak summary in Shakespeare's own life. It can't be proved, but to judge from the surrounding plays, *Hamlet*, *Macbeth*, *Troilus and Cressida*, and *Timon of Athens*, I subscribe to the belief that these works represent a dark period in Shakespeare's personal life which his artistic life of course reflected; it's not surprising that all his conclusions and summaries about living were very darkly colored. From this we know that he emerged into a final kind of acceptance, as witness *The Winter's Tale* and finally *The Tempest*. This is assumed to be the romantic view of Shakespeare's life, but it's also, I think, a realistic view. All men in the course of their experience come to some kind of blank wall where they have to ask themselves, "Is it all worth-while?" Shakespeare, even in *Lear*, talks about "this life's sweetness." He recognized the fact that this is the only life we have to live, and we don't wish to surrender it foolishly; but at the same time, the contemplation of it at a certain period in a man's life can be very grim.

I still grapple with the values of this play which have already been expressed in thousands of ways. The actor must, of course, tackle it from the point of view of how to do it on the stage. I found that it was necessary for me to cope with every scene as a complete entity in itself. The first scene, with all its expense of energy, was for me a whole evening's work, so to speak. Not that I felt that I had done my job at the end of that scene, but that what I expressed had to be expressed fully. There was no saving of one's self. The explosions toward Cordelia, toward Kent, the bitter summations to Burgundy and France, and the disposing of Cordelia all demanded an inordinate amount of energy that *had* to be expended. The sense of loss through my own deed, the sense of something gone out of my life was the springboard for a kind of haunted feeling that led me into my next scene, culminating in the curse of Goneril, an expenditure of energy which I have never had to use before in any play. Then the beautiful little scene that follows, almost wordless, absentminded, with the Fool, a scene of almost hopeless hope, snatching at love and deluding myself that I will find it with Regan. And then, of course, the great moment where I begin to perceive that I am not and never was a King, that fundamentally I am a poor old man, when the two daughters tear at me with their suggestions of how little I *need* in the way of companionship, attention, and attendance. This is the first great, firm realization in Lear's mind that he has, and is, nothing. That word "nothing" is very haunting as it occurs throughout the play. "Nothing will come of nothing." The realization of his "nothingness" leads to the action of giving himself to the storm (the tragic hero's act), going out into a savage world and taking the consequences of anything that will happen. Here again, there can be no saving of oneself on the part of the actor. Almost immediately, with no more than a breath of intermission, he comes directly into it with "Blow, winds, and crack your cheeks." This, the scene with Regan, and the curse of Goneril, are perhaps the most physically demanding moments of the play.

Consider the superficial technical demands of that "Blow, winds, and crack your cheeks." It is obviously a huge speech, needing one vast exertion of energy. I expended enough for the whole scene, you might say, in the very first long speech, but then Shakespeare provided a fairly short speech on the part of the Fool to interrupt my ravings (Fool: O nuncle, court holy-water in a dry house, etc.) and that speech came to me like a vacation right on the stage, so that I found it possible for me to simply rest, collapse; that moment provided me with an opportunity to recover my own strength before I launched into the next section of the scene. It makes one appreciate Shakespeare's craftsmanship. It was as if he realized that no actor could carry on beyond a certain point.

We played *King Lear* in two halves; at the end of the first half, there's no question I was fairly exhausted. I even have pictures to prove it. The second part of the play began with the final hovel scene where Lear is going over the borderline to madness and where he arraigns the two wicked daughters whose images he summons up before him. They become intensely real. It's a device that Shakespeare often uses, the reality of the fantasy, a phantasmagorical physicality; for example, Juliet in the potion scene, Macbeth and the dagger, Clarence's dream in *Richard the Third*. In the course of this hovel scene, Lear, literally exhausted, falls asleep and has to be carried off and taken care of. Luckily, for me there's a long intermission at this point in the play after which I come on crowned with flowers and play the "mad" scene with the blinded Gloucester and Edgar as Poor Tom.

The final scene in which I bring on Cordelia dead in my arms is perhaps the final expenditure of energy, physically, for the actor: the "Howl, howl, howl" an almost animal cry in the wilderness. To me it said for the last time that this business of life is hardly worthwhile, that there's nothing left for us but to "howl" our "way to dusty death." Mistakenly or not, as I've said before, I reject any discovery at the end that Cordelia lives, that for a moment life flutters back into her lips. His question to Edgar, "Do you see this?" is a last kind of communication with a human being which intends to say, "Are you aware, young man, what kind of life you are in for, of what faces you? It's *nothing*. It ends in ignominious death, and all I have in my last moments is the memory of this beautiful person whom I rejected; and that's all." "Look there, look there" at the end does not mean, "Behold, she is alive again, and I die comforted in the realization of it," but simply "I accuse you, you gods, and you elements, and you men, of having destroyed the worth of life!" I confess it's a hopeless kind of resolution, but I could see nothing that warranted anything else.

But curiously, and this is the quality of tragedy which undoubtedly we must discuss in talking about *Lear*, I found the doing of it strangely uplifting. In my own way, I came to curse and remained to pray. Perhaps it was simply the expenditure of energy toward an uplifting conclusion. *Lear* ends in any way but uplifting, and yet the doing of a tragedy is something which carries with it its own purgation. So that I remember distinctly that at the end of the performances of Lear, even though they may not have been of the highest attainment, my feeling "that's a job well done," and that in a way carries with it an uplifting quality. *Lear* attempts everything, both the character and the play. It represents Shakespeare's conscious attempt to put his own life on the line, to say "here it is, here is the life we live, here is the society we exist in, and I intend to show it in all of its horror, at the same time not ignoring the fact that life may be illuminated by the character of good people along the way." I agree with Hazlitt that this was *the* play in which Shakespeare withheld nothing. Perhaps this is what prompted me to say to Alan Fletcher at the beginning, "we go for broke." We withhold nothing. As good a way, I think, of embarking on a tragedy as any.

In words that are both baffling and illuminating, Lear at the outset forecasts his tragic course: "Meantime we shall express our darker purpose."

What is this "darker purpose"? Almost immediately the actor is forced to decide for himself whether this seemingly casual announcement is indeed casual or is in fact related to the character's profoundest intention. Set a poet to catch a poet: Dame Edith Sitwell has commented upon the numerously reiterated uses of the word "dark," and with that clue the actor gropes toward a fundamental insight, namely the presence, or immanence, of the *unconscious* in everything that Shakespeare writes. Edgar, wrapped in the mysterious persona of Poor Tom, says, "Nero is an angler in the lake of darkness" and as we descend into the final hovel scene: "Child Rowland to the dark tower came." This last became for us a kind of terrible summons, the very core meaning of the play, namely that *everyone* in it was descending into some kind of lake of darkness—*all* the characters. No other play that Shakespeare or anybody else ever wrote is more saturated with the tragic. Every character without exception is tragic; together they seem to embody the very nature of tragedy.

The characters are caught in necessity, all of them. One by one, in more or less degree, they recognize that they are subject to a personal necessity from which they cannot escape. Each one has his own "dark tower." This is what creates a tragic atmosphere around them. Goneril—a fascinating character in her own right. She cannot help herself; she is impaled on the compulsion to achieve power, as well as to achieve love in whatever twisted way she can, and this gives everything that she does a "darkly" tragic quality.

The Fool and Kent *cannot help themselves.* They, too, are conditioned, forced, into what they *do* by the deepest necessity of their natures, namely, their fidelity. One by one, *every* character can be examined from the point of view of this touchstone of *necessity.*

In working on it I recognized also that there was another element, particularly as applied to the action of Lear himself, and that was the element of mystery. I had the feeling that there was something about the whole action of the play which came out of mystery and went again into mystery at the end of the play. I had in mind a comparison, a parallel, between this play and those Chinese scrolls which reveal a painting as you open them; there's one particularly that has to do with the Island of the Storks. As it begins unrolling, it shows you a kind of atmospheric nothingness which develops into a view of water on which perhaps a random piece of seaweed or a land plant is floating, and as it unfolds, suddenly you see one stork flying in the direction of the scroll's unfolding, joined eventually by another and another and another until finally you come to the island itself which is inhabited by storks, a multitude of them. The scroll continues to unfold and it takes you away from the island again onto the sea. The mist closes in on the scene, and the storks are no longer visible, and all you have is seaweed and a final fog at the end of the scroll. Well, I used to think of the whole play as taking shape in Shakespeare's mind very much in that manner.

I once heard the great Russian Jewish actor, Mikhoels, speak about *his* "collision" with *Lear*. He had just come to this country, to California, during the war to make some personal appearances in support of our alliance with Russia at that time, and he spoke to us as actors. One of the things he drew my own attention to—at that time, of course, I didn't know I was ever going to do Lear myself—I found very stimulating. Concerning that first critical scene in which Lear divides his kingdom, Mikhoels dismissed immediately any notion of this being a simple device of getting the play on its way as in the old fairy tale of a king dividing up his kingdom among three children. He said that his own sense of cause and effect would not permit him to think that it was as simple as that.

I know that during my own study I was instinctively guided by a feeling, or perhaps I hoped for a certain logic so that what I wanted to emerge, and what I think finally did, was a clarity. People who remember our production will tell you that they found themselves, for the first time, really understanding what was happening on the stage. My own approach to the work was one that I brought to every play. I was oddly "suspicious" of it, as if it was a trap set to catch me. My habit was to "stalk" the text as it sat on my table and without reading it, to instinctively take the measure of it and allow it to take the measure of me. Eventually, this instinctive movement was to emerge as a more or less complete identification with the play. My association with this role became a kind of supreme test, I think, of everything that I represented to myself: a test of my life work, my maturity. The word "test" is very important.

It may be that this was the only play I've ever done that I've designed from the inside. I had to think it through. I asked myself the usual questions: what is the center of this character; where does it come from; where is it going; and actually the things we've already talked about: the feeling of mystery surrounding the play, the lonely working out of the necessity of this tragic character from beginning to end; the realization also of his climaxes, of his high points, of the moments when as an actor I had to let myself go completely and then find places in the play—and this is interesting—where I would have to recover my strength.

In *Hamlet*, Shakespeare asked the unavoidable question for any sensitive human being, "What am I? What am I worth?" or as Goddard phrased it, "For what was such a man made?" Lear asks the same question more darkly and in an even more demanding, exacting context. Lear plunges deliberately into evil in order to test his own ability to survive, to test his character as a man, to fetch up out of chaos whatever meaning there is in the whole adventure of life. And that word "test" in its very nature is the touchstone of *Lear*. It provides the justification for the story all along the line. In the "mad scene" with Gloucester, which is in some ways the most blindingly clear scene in the play, he says, "They told me I was everything. 'Tis a lie—I am not ague-proof," to me a terribly wrenching and tragic remark. This, while not representing the whole search of the play, is a gnawing question throughout. Earlier Lear asks in his confrontation with Goneril, "Does any here know me? This is not Lear./. . .Who is it that can tell me who I am?" He has been accustomed, not only by his own actions and behavior, but by the encouragement of all the people around him to believe he was a certain and definite entity. He was Lear. And suddenly he finds that he's not; and he is plunged into the kind of confusion and storm of the mind that is echoed by the larger storm, the physical storm in which he finds himself raging.

All the things we've been talking about: the search for the Spine, the use of the Self, the support of Objects, all these things, I can say as an actor, are tested here, tested by the actor's collision with the play.

As I waited there for my first entrance, what was going through my mind, both as actor and as the Lear played by this actor, was something like this: "I have arrived at a certain point in my life where I have to discover for myself what I am. In spite of everything that I have felt so far, in spite of everything that people tell me, I *am determined to test myself* against whatever ultimate values there are in life. I'm going to take the extreme course of deliberately dividing up my kingdom, giving away my power. At the same time asserting my personal right to kingship. I can't give up my personality as a king, but I do intend to surrender all the visible appurtenances and evidences of royalty. This is an incredible act. No one will really believe it." The people who surround him, even the people who are closest to him—the Fool, Cordelia, Kent—cannot be expected to understand what's in the depths of his mind when he walks up to the throne. "But I'm going to do it in order to test what I really am; how the man that I am faces up to whatever may result from my action." For me as an actor this decision was a conscious choice, but I don't think that it's arrived at by Lear himself in any conscious, mechanical way. I construe it as a test which he cannot deny himself, self-imposed, and this represents the "darker purpose" which persists throughout the play.

You recall the old story of King Canute who was repeatedly assured by his courtiers that he was "everything"—omnipotent. He has them carry his throne down to the seashore; there he commands the waves to stand back. Of course, they don't, and "so much for my omnipotence," says Canute.

There is an element of pathos in that first scene, of course, as he asks for some expression of love from his daughters; Goneril obliges him by making a fulsome statement of her love which is imitated and even outdone by Regan. I assumed in my playing that Lear recognizes that these are formal expressions, even recitations, that they are necessary as a carrying out of the form of his request, and that what he is really thinking about (again the "darker purpose") is what will happen as a consequence of giving away his kingdom.

Then suddenly Cordelia doesn't play the game. Upon which his customary, explosive, even tyrannical nature asserts itself, simply because he has been defied and flouted by his most loving daughter in open court; as a man accustomed to having what he wants, he finds himself suddenly turning against the best thing in his life. There is pathos in this. He asks for the test; and yet when it comes almost immediately through the opposition of Cordelia's nobility and honesty, he can't take it; he flies out at her and at everyone who supports her, especially Kent; and thus the tragedy is precipitated. It's a very difficult point to clinch in the performance, but it's there for the actor who plays Lear to try for. I am not sure we ever really solved this thing, but at any rate, the play develops from the major premise of that first scene. The world expressed itself now in all of its characteristic qualities: Good and Evil. From this time on, Lear bears the burden of his own deed. He finds himself extending the test. He deliberately exposes himself (someone has said the essence of the play might be the word "exposure") to the forces of Nature, as well as of human nature.

Once having given himself to the flames, as it were, he is his own sacrifice; he accepts his tragic necessity. In Norse poetry, the Hero is often characterized as "doom-eager," a wonderfully double-barreled phrase which suggests that the Hero not only recognizes his fate, but challenges it, surrenders to it. Lear expresses this idea himself: "Upon such sacrifices, my Cordelia,/The gods themselves throw incense," which suggests that he is aware of his own tragic, "doom-eager" character. The particular "pride" or Lear's fatal flaw is a compulsion to match his will against Nature herself. Another way of pursuing "darker purpose."

The storm: it's as if in the midst of it he is saying, "Through my own deed I have asked for everything that is happening to me, but 'Pour on, I will endure.'" The very nature of this defiance is the working out of the original test that he has imposed on himself, a test not only of physical but spiritual endurance. The titanic character of the man precipitates titanic consequences.

In this connection Mikhoels suggested an idea that I find fascinating. Lear is fourscore and ten and going through situations and debacles that would have killed an old man right at the outset. But Lear refuses to die. It's as if he says, "I will consent to die only when I find out what this is all about." It's that kind of will that keeps him alive. He could only go to pieces in madness, the only way out. Perhaps this will, expressed in the words "Pour on, I will endure," is all the "Spine" the actor needs. It's only at the end of the play when he finds the love of Cordelia again, and when he accuses Nature and God for the last time, that he surrenders to death. He himself wills to enter the tomb. That was Mikhoel's idea. Lear simply says, "Now is the time. I've had it. Sufficient. Enough," and he deliberately ceases to live. It's a fascinating idea.

There's another significant fact. Lear is old and yet fundamentally untried. This test he undergoes will establish in him the very first beginning of a manhood that he has never really possessed, a simple manhood. It is finally won through love. He begins to perceive a distinction between the things he has valued as important and those which have no importance at all. At the end, when Cordelia asks, "Shall we not see these daughters and these sisters?" he dismisses it: "No, no, no, no! Come, let's away to prison./We two alone will sing like birds i' th' cage." All life, all power is focused and narrowed down to the simple, communicating act of love.

A sense of authority is something that Lear possesses throughout the play, even in his madness. He dominates the play because of his determination to pursue the course I have described. The first scene is authority itself; here his tyrannical will is fully exposed. From then on, we see that same will undermined by certain doubts, even regrets. It's love, really, that is working at him, but he doesn't admit it. When he's told that the Fool has sorrowed since Cordelia's departure for France, he flies out at the man who says it with "No more of that!" And then immediately he relents, "I have noted it well."

There's this marvelous sensitiveness in Lear which is at the same time subject to his natural extroverted and tyrannical quality. It's not for nothing that people follow him with love. Those men around him love him. He is close to them, and they are close to him. The Fool especially and Kent. Both of them are symbols of it—Kent says, "You have that in your countenance which I would fain call master." A man like Kent doesn't simply bow before an unqualified tyrant. Lear was a professional king. He has had to rule. He's a good ruler, and everyone knows it. He has solidified Britain just as he is now about to tear the whole thing apart and divide it up. There must have been very good reasons for everyone accepting him as their logical monarch. He is Britain. He is the kingdom. And now he tears himself apart; this is the disruption of the play, the disruption of the first scene.

The presence of Kent in that scene is one that reflects the more obviously sympathetic qualities of Lear. Kent loves his King, and he cannot help himself. He cannot do otherwise. The picture of this shadow of love following Lear throughout the play is very beautiful; at the end when Kent says, "My master calls me; I must not say no," there again is a recognition of tragic necessity. He too "consents" to die. He is a much lesser Lear.

It's up to the actor playing Lear, I think, to realize this quality and to suggest his feeling of the subtext. For example, the moment when he asks Cordelia in the first scene to say how much she loves him, it's a moment of tenderness and humor. It's as if he says to himself, "I know what you say is going to be genuine, from the heart." Then suddenly everything is destroyed, transformed.

The Fool's affection for Lear is of a double nature, different from Kent's: full of love and tenderness on the one hand, caustic and lacerating on the other. It's the psychoanalyst's job of saying to his "patient" not only "I love you and I want to bring you through this condition," but also "You made your bed, realize it, now lie in it because it's the only way that you will be able to regain

As Falstaff in the Brandeis University production of *Henry IV, Part I*,
directed by Peter Sander, 1970.

As Grumio in the American Shakespeare Festival production of *Taming of the Shrew*, 1956.

As Lear in the American Shakespeare Festival production of *King Lear*, 1963.

The American Shakespeare Festival production of *A Midsummer Night's Dream*, 1958. L. to r.: Hiram Sherman, Morris Carnovsky.

your health." It was always a kind of illumination to the person playing the Fool to realize what his function was in that scene with Lear immediately following the cursing of Goneril: the beginning of this double-edged thing. When they understood what the scene was about, they used to love it. We both loved it, the simplicity, the humor, and a certain "lost" quality. At the end of my speech to Regan and Goneril when Lear holds back his tears:

> this heart
> Shall break into a hundred thousand flaws
> Or ere I'll weep.

I arranged for my right hand to be hanging loose while I faced Regan. In the meantime the Fool has approached me and placed his hand inside mine; I turn to him and say, "O fool, I shall go mad." That simple thing, a little spark of activity, was all in the nature of defining the reality of the characters and their relationship to each other.

The end of the Fool's role, "And I'll go to bed at noon," is utterly simple and perfect. His function is over. He joins, in a sense, the feeling of Lear at the end—Lear's hopelessness. It's as if his job is finished; it's over, he can't go on any further. Incidentally, it's John Gielgud's belief that possibly in Shakespeare's time the part of Cordelia was doubled with the part of the Fool since the two never appear together. But I don't think we need to think about it in that way. His sudden disappearance is eloquent in itself: the weariness of it and again the mystery.

But we must not forget that these simple, human relationships are laid out on an immense canvas. I love what Harbage has written in his introduction to the play:

> Lear's anguish now represents for us Man's horror and sense of helplessness at the discovery of evil—the infiltration of animality in the human world, naked cruelty and appetite. It is a fissure that threatens to widen infinitely, and we see Lear at the center of turbulence as it works its breakage in minds, in families, in nations, in the heavens themselves, interacting in dreadful concatenation . . . He batters himself to pieces against the fact of evil. Granted that its disruptive power has been unleashed by his own error, so that error itself partakes of evil, as he is shudderingly aware, yet he remains the great antagonist. Falsity, cruelty, injustice, corruption—their appalling forms swirl about him in phantasmic patterns. His instinct is to rip them from the universe, to annihilate these things. His charges of universal hypocrisy: "handy-dandy, which is the justice, which is the thief?"—his denial of human responsibility: "None does offend, none—I say none!"—his indictment of life itself:
>
> > Thou know'st, the first time that we smell the air
> > We wawl and cry—
>
> cancel their own nihilism, because they sound no acquiescence. Lear is the voice of protest. The grandeur of his spirit supplies the impotence of his body as he opposes to evil all that is left him to oppose—his molten indignation, his huge invectives, his capacity for feeling pain.*

---

*Ibid., pages 26, 27.

When I say that Lear is his own sacrifice, he seems almost the sacrifice of Man, lifted up to our view by Shakespeare himself.

The words that Harbage quotes are uttered by Lear during his madness; for me this madness was rather the realm of "amazing discovery." It was as if having crossed into madness itself, everything to Lear became new in its own right. The fact, for example, that Poor Tom expressed himself with a kind of abandoned, unbridled imaginativeness, intrigued me as Lear beyond anything that I had ever experienced. It was as if I was saying to him "I know you; what were you before you became mad? You fascinate me." I call him "my philosopher." I want him with me; when they try to separate us, I resist. I invented a kind of mad dance, a trio involving Poor Tom, the Fool, and myself, suggesting my complete identification with Tom's madness, anticipating his very thinking. We were together in madness, the three of us. I wanted to be a citizen of his country, to be with him, sharing his condition, whatever it was. Lear doesn't think of himself as mad. He simply thinks of himself as entering a new country, making huge, new discoveries.

Eventually the sheer weariness of the whole experience overcomes him and he falls asleep, but the extraordinary energy, the virility, with which he persists in asking the question, whether mad or sane, "What am I? Who am I?" repeats itself again and again.

When he enters later, alone, crowned with flowers, his madness takes the form of an almost unbearable clarity. He perceives in life many overtones of sexual depravity, so that he finds one name for all women and that is "lust"; and one name for all men and that is "violence." Even the blindness of Gloucester is treated by him with a certain amount of cruelty and objectivity. He says, "if you don't have any eyes, 'look with thine ears.' "

Eventually I broke through to a deeper compassion for Gloucester:

I know thee well enough: thy name is Gloucester
Thou must be patient.

It's the same patience that he begged of the gods in the earlier scene with Regan:

You heavens, give me that patience, patience I need.

Pulling all of this together was more complex than my work in *The Merchant of Venice*. In Shylock I found a very convenient, stimulating Spine. With Lear it was different. The seach for the Spine in Lear was double-edged. You couldn't nail it down. There were so many complications. The main Spine, however, emerged from the statement, "Pour on, I will endure." This statement supports the actor playing Lear in all of his activities, the violent activities that are his response to the whole disruption of Nature and society as symbolized by the storm. At the same time, the quiet center in the midst of this hurricane is the necessity of Lear to find out what he is, to penetrate to the very center of his being; the search eventuates with his discovery and his acceptance of the fact that within this king, there lies waiting a simple man, a human being.

Perhaps these two intentions come together between the "mad scene" and the awakening scene, because Lear is a different person after he emerges from insanity into the scene with Cordelia. Up to that time, he has encountered everything that happens to him with his characteristic violence of temper and firmness of will. Perhaps he is chastened by misfortune, although I hesitate to use the term, because fundamentally in Lear there still burns the desire to test the values of life right to the very end. Even in the last scene I found myself accusing the Maker over the body of Cordelia, accusing not only men of this death, but accusing the God who made these men. Again the mystery of things; in those last moments I felt I was emerging out of that Island of the Storks back into the sea that surrounds us all. It's a terribly complicated play. And yet the actor has got to find the simplicities that make it possible for him to act from one scene to another. I chose to think about each scene as being a play unto itself.

For example, take the moment in the first scene when I turn to Cordelia and ask her,

> what can you say to draw
> A third more opulent than your sisters?

She answers, "Nothing." What goes on in his mind before he repeats her "nothing"? Is it the knowledge that the whole court is there, silent, watching, listening, waiting for my reaction because they know my violent nature? I try to control it, as I say, almost with the suggestion of a joke: "Nothing will come of nothing. Speak again." And then Cordelia responds: (paraphrasing) "Why do my sisters promise what they do, when they owe so much more allegiance to their husbands, as I will when I marry?" Inside of me as I listen, and the court watches, I try to control my desire to fly out at her. I ask, " 'But goes thy heart with this?' Do you really *mean* this?" She answers, "Ay, my good lord." And I'm still struggling; I want to hold on. I want her to change her mind. She is exposing me. She is not going through with the game, the formality, as her sisters did. I was indifferent to them in a sense, but I'm not indifferent to her. I was about to give her a third of the kingdom. "So young, and so untender?" And she counters in the only way she can: "So young, my lord, and true." The scene begins to threaten: " 'Let it be so.' If that's how you want to play it, 'thy truth then be thy dower.' That's what you're going to get from me, this empty truth that you're talking about." Then, of course, he can't hold on to himself, and he breaks forth with a vow, the alienating curse of Cordelia. But I would point out, the things that happen occur in between the words; underneath the scene:

the whole sense of his kingship crumbling in those few moments; the attack on his pride, on his plan, his "darker purpose"; and, consciously or not, he goes to his doom at this moment of eternally rejecting Cordelia. Then Kent comes, of course, to the protection of Cordelia, and Lear banishes him, too.

It's almost impossible in thinking about *King Lear* to divorce one's imagination from the mighty creations of other poets and painters. It has often been said that *Lear* is on the same level as Beethoven's *Missa Solemnis*. The mere mention of that gives a certain lift and impulse to an actor's imagination. Also in painting: I found myself thinking a lot about *The Last Judgement* by Michelangelo. In fact, there was one embodiment in this painting which seized on me. That was the figure of the damned creature with a hand covering half his face, whose attitude I actually imitated in one section of the play. The terror, the loneliness, and the utter horror and impotence of this character seemed to me to symbolize the condition of Lear's mind in the midst of the storm and in the madness that ensued, so that at one point in the hovel scene, I found myself utterly abandoning my imagination to the idea of perdition, and I incorporated the gesture of this character who is damned.

Once you commit yourself to a play, everything that happens seems to collaborate with the intention of producing that image on the stage. It occurred to me that the sound of a drum, a mysterious, muffled drum might be heard way off stage: perhaps Lear's heart; perhaps the footsteps of fate; perhaps, to let it be clear, a distant call to action, the suggestion that Lear is following "a different drummer" as it were. That's an imaginative kind of thing which we didn't choose to do, but it remained an image that stimulated me.

When Edgar appears for the first time as Poor Tom, and I stare at him, it's borne in on me that this is "unaccomodated man," naked; everything and nothing. It's a tremendous realization: "this is all of us. I'm no different from him." We worked on a sound for that moment from the orchestra, a sort of crescendo which I puncture by snapping my fingers as if my worldly intelligence had snapped. Right there was *the turning point into madness*. What I wanted was something like the effect of that broken string in the second act of Chekhov's *Cherry Orchard*.

In the final analysis, however, nothing takes the place of the actor's inner passion to merge with the character that Shakespeare has given him. He identifies through sympathy and imagination with what he finds in the play. Eventually everything is discharged through his own sense of Self. It's *my own* frustration; it's *my own* indignation; it's *my own* anger; it's *my own* seeking; it's *my own* dawning sympathy with the world, with the "Poor naked wretches . . . That bide the pelting of this pitiless storm." There's a peculiar kind of inner logic that extends throughout the play; and against this you test the validity of the outer image that you've chosen. In the moment I just quoted I was helped, of course, by the progressive deterioration of the clothes I was wearing, the reduction to bereavement, the bereft quality of Lear in the storm; and then finally by the simplicity of the costume that I wore when coming out of madness into a recognition of my daughter's return.

The designer at Stratford, Will Steven Armstrong, saw the play in the terms that Alan Fletcher and I had conceived it; and he was able to dress me very helpfully. He simply designed three versions of the same costume: one of total magnificence; the middle one a somewhat worn imitation of the first; and finally the third which was very tattered and torn. He also designed the set; and it was by far the finest set I have ever played in for *King Lear*. I remember, in my first meeting with him, I asked, "Have you any notion of the style in which you intend to design?" and he pulled out of his pocket a photograph of a corroded piece of iron and said, "That's the beginning of what I'm thinking about." There was a real meeting of minds about this conception.

One of the things that helped me most in doing Lear was what I might call a sense of music. For instance in the stunning speech to Goneril and Regan, "O reason not the need!" there are accumulations of feelings and pauses, there are moments when the thought is brooded over before it charges on. There are moments when it rises to a climax and dies away into nothingness. There is a coda, "O fool, I shall go mad!" All these things enter into the actual saying of these speeches. In the curse of Goneril, "Hear, Nature, hear; dear goddess, hear," there sounds an appeal that is, to me, musical.

Suspend thy purpose if thou didst intend
To make this creature fruitful.

The lines are laid out musically throughout the speech; and all of it is upheld by the fundamental Action which surges within it: to eradicate her forever, to destroy her, root and branch. At the end of the play kneeling by the dead Cordelia, Lear points to Edgar to get his attention before saying, "Do you see this?" That connection with Edgar; half mad, half removed from earth already, half prepared to "enter the tomb"; that is, in a sense, musical, all sustained by the inner stimuli of Action leading to Emotion. Once you sense it, you respond to it, you repeat it. That is the business of the actor.

A last word on "Actor's Sympathy"—what is it? Perhaps it is simply to be understood as the relation of the Self with the Object—in essence an act of love. At the conclusion of *Lear* I love that moment with Edgar: "Do you see this? . . . Look there . . . Look there." The word is *look*. We can say that the whole interpenetration with a role like Lear is a series of fits and starts of discovery, as if the actor is exclaiming with startled, new-found vision, "How about *this*! And *this*! *Look* at this! My God, and *this*!" I think I can say that the very examination of our capabilities as actors in the Group Theatre was an act of love. And fundamentally, that's how I still think about everything that an actor does with all his truth and depth. An act of love.

PHOTO CREDITS:

Eileen Darby, 89; Paul Duckworth, 20, 91; Fred Fehl, 197 (top left); Friedman-Abeles, 182, 197 (right); Serge Gorlanoff, 165; Don Ornitz, 114 (top); William L. Smith, 113; Talbot, 6, 148 (top right); Alfredo Valente, 73, 74, 75, 130; Vandamm, 60, 61, 148 (top left).